Lost in the Stars of the Southern Cross: The Making of a Brazilianist

Lost in the Stars of the Southern Cross: The Making of a Brazilianist

Jordan M. Young
Professor Emeritus,
Pace University

ISBN 978-1-312-03263-7

Acknowledgements

I thank Patricia Taylor, Ryan Gyukeri, Adam Lang, and Margy Levine Young for help with this manuscript.

Dedications

To Dionir, without whom this book would not have happened.

To Margy and JM, for the encouragement.

Table of Contents

MAP OF BRAZIL

Chapter 1. Leaving Home (1939-41)

In February 1939, I enrolled as a freshman at the University of Illinois Champaign-Urbana campus, with a major in Latin American history. To make ends meet I cut the pages of uncut foreign periodicals on the C floor of the university library. That job, to show you how times have changed, was under the auspices of the National Youth Administration, one of President Franklin Delano Roosevelt's initiatives to keep people like myself from entering the work force during the Great Depression. Receiving the magnificent sum of 25 cents an hour and working four or five hours each week I made just enough to eat. A hamburger and milk shake were 25 cents in those days.

One of the periodicals that I cut was the English language

On the Main Street of Champaign-Urbana, Illinois.

edition of Escola Livre de Sociologia e Política de São Paulo, Brazil (the Free School of Sociology and Politics of São Paulo). I remembered sitting on the floor and being fascinated by the description of the school. To me, an extremely bored student, it seemed as though São Paulo would be the perfect place to spend my junior year. Movies of the time like "Flying Down to Rio" and "Copacabana" and stars like Carmen Miranda, Ginger Rogers, and Fred Astaire flickered across my adolescent mind and clinched my decision.

I fell in with some art students at the University of Illinois.

Getting into the University of São Paulo was a Catch-22 story. Brazil at the time did not admit foreigners or even permit them to study at their universities. The University of São Paulo was supported by the state and by the tax dollars of their citizens. As a foreigner, I did not pay taxes and could not enter. They were amazed that an American was trying to get into their university. Then the negotiations began.

They thought I was, like all Americans, rich beyond all calculations. How do you tell people you are not wealthy? I gave up early in the game. They said as money didn't mean anything to me they were going to let me in as an "*ouvinte livre*," literally a "free listener," but also one who had all the privileges of a paying student. After a few letters and one frantic telegram telling me that Portuguese would be required (which I ignored), I made plans with the expectation that my four semesters of Spanish would get me by. I would not get official credit for the courses, but would take the exams. That was perfectly okay with me, and if I had to pretend that I was wealthy, that was also okay. They promised to inform the University of Illinois that I was a student at the University of São Paulo.

New York Days

My parents lived in Manhattan, where the boat was scheduled to depart. While wandering about New York during the days preceding the trip, I noticed a Brazilian flag flying from the second floor of 551 Fifth Avenue and promptly went in. There I met José Garrido Torres, a young Brazilian economist studying for a Masters Degree at New York University while working with the Brazilian Government Trade Bureau. We chatted for about an hour and he roundly approved of my plans to go to Brazil. We became fast friends, a friendship that persisted over decades, when we would meet in different positions. He became head of the Economic Council under Brazilian President Juscelino Kubitschek and later still in 1964 he was named President of BNDE, Brazil's National Economic Development Bank.

My passport photograph, 1941.

TIME magazine would be our lifeline to the U.S.A, and I had the brilliant idea of going to TIME magazine and asking if I could get the student edition of the magazine while I was in Brazil. A student subscription cost $1.75 while an airmail edition cost $10. I wanted the student price for the airmail edition. I was a student, I figured.

I remember wearing my leather jacket and being rather apprehensive about what I was doing as the receptionist on the street level floor directed me to the 17th floor of the TimeLife Building. The secretary must have been very nice because she sent me to talk to Richard P. Callahan, who was in charge of circulation for Latin America. He listened carefully as I explained why I wanted the reduced student price for the airmail edition. I was going to be a student at the University of São Paulo and therefore I thought I was eligible.

After hearing my story, he said: "I'll tell you what I am going to do for you. You go down to Brazil and send me detailed reports on how *TIME* is displayed on the newsstands. If I like it I'll consider sending you a free subscription of *TIME*." I was thrilled and jubilant. I took that suggestion as a command if I ever heard one.

The Boat Trip

On November 8, 1941, a young, very innocent, brash, naïve American (me) boarded the S.S. Uruguay at pier 32. Despite the fact that it was a nasty drizzly evening, everyone in my family gathered, some in tears, to wave goodbye to me. My mother was unsure whether she would ever see me again. Some of this feeling was probably due to my only having a one way ticket to Rio de Janeiro, as I didn't have enough for the round trip. She most certainly would never see the same person who sailed that night.

Life aboard the S.S. Uruguay had a romantic quality to it. The tourist class passengers would gather at the stern of the ship, especially in the evening. Once we reached the tropics we were warned by the purser that the red glow from a cigarette butt could be seen for miles and that we might be attacked by German U-boats. He was quick to add that we shouldn't worry as the U.S.A. was a neutral country. Twelve blissful days went by quickly, without any signs of U-boats.

I knew one other person traveling on the boat. Harold Midkiff, who I had met in Washington two weeks earlier, was on his way to a posting as an American naval attaché in Brazil[1].

Also among the passengers were Kay, Katya, and Kay, a dance trio whose most popular act was to throw the woman between the two men. It played big in the night clubs of Urca (a neighborhood in Rio) and the casino in Santos (the port of São Paulo). They took a liking to me and when we arrived in Rio they had me sit at their table at the Cassino de Urca, where I had my first drink of scotch. They seemed to know every performer in Rio and I was introduced to all of them, which seemed an interesting way of getting to know the country. Years later I remember meeting an elegant matron who was a member of the garden club of Larchmont, New York. She admitted to having been the Katya who had been flung across the stage by the two men.

---

[1] In 2009, the *Folha de São Paulo* interviewed him about his experiences in Brazil during war.

The last night on the S.S. Uruguay on the way to Rio de Janeiro. My traveling companion (left) and the purser (center) were astounded at my appetite.

An attractive woman from the Amazon offered to teach me Portuguese on the trip, which I accepted. A man named Alpha Jewel, who had only three fingers on his right hand, offered me a free ride from Rio to São Paulo in his brand new 1942 Chevy. Again I accepted, gratefully so because it meant I would save about $30 from my meager savings.

The utter chaos of the arrival in Rio de Janeiro was classically Brazilian. A band of music greeted the passengers and the guys huffed and puffed their way through the smart tunes of day. Though we docked in the early afternoon it was nearly midnight before our luggage was cleared through customs. The confusion in the barn-like shed where all the baggage was collected was colossal. In the distance, I could see the huge clock on the building of the *Noite* newspaper at the foot of Avenida Rio Branco, the main street of downtown Rio. This image burned itself into my mind. We were at the rundown, seedy part of the avenue. When my passport was finally stamped, it bore the date November 19, 1941.

The Car Trip

Finally, it was time to get into the 1942 Chevy and start the drive to São Paulo. It was a nine-hour, 350 mile trip over many unpaved roads and I got my first taste of the power and jealously of the Brazilian states in those days. States' rights were a fact of life. Every state was jealous of their rights, one of the many problems caused by a touchy system of federalism. Each state was almost a country to itself. They had their own state militias that were basically armies. The Getúlio Vargas dictatorship made efforts to take away some of this power, but only succeeded with smaller and weaker states, leaving states like São Paulo and Minas Gerais relatively untouched.

How exaggerated was the power of the states that when we left the Federal District of Rio de Janeiro there was a road block and a guard station. We pulled over and the guards started to search the car and ask for documentation. Alpha Jewel asked that I show them my freshly minted passport and it was okay to pass.

After a few more miles, we were in the state of Rio de Janeiro and ran into the next guard station. This time the Rio de Janeiro State Police stopped us and we went through the same routine.

Alpha Jewel and the car which I unknowingly helped smuggle into Brazil, en route to Rio de Janeiro.

The ubiquitous oxcarts which acted as a popular form of transportation.

Again, Mr. Jewel asked me to show them my passport and again we were able to proceed. After few hours driving we hit the border of São Paulo and the whole routine started all over again. Inspections, talk, talk, I showed them my passport, and we were clear to go through.

Only forty years later did I learn that I helped to smuggle a car into Brazil. In 1980, through a curious chain of events, I was asked to read some documents which Princeton University had acquired from the Rubber Development Corporation, one of those World War II agencies the United States created to help supply raw materials for the war effort. Princeton had bought these documents with the idea that they might be of some use to graduate students and I was asked to check them out to see if this might be the case. As I went over the documents that day I read the name of Alpha Jewel, a name that for me jumped out of a letter. A Rubber Development Corporation official had written that Alpha Jewel was a notorious automobile smuggler and had offered ten cars - which they had indignantly refused - to the Corporation.

Blissfully unaware of this and showing my passport at every stop, Alpha Jewel and I continued our drive to São Paulo. Oxcarts were in evidence as we stopped in a small town to eat lunch. The incredible screeching noise from the wooden wheels announced their presence long before you saw them. It was total night when we finally arrived. Alpha Jewel told me as I did not have a place to stay, the first night in São Paulo would be on him.

He added that he'd be sending up a young lady to my hotel room. I tried to explain that it was not necessary. Fresh from the University of Illinois, I was not sure what he meant and sex was not something that I had much experience with. I was just plain scared; my sexual experience had been on the limited side, once to be exact. But he insisted. At about 11 o'clock, there was a timid knock on the door. I opened it and a pretty young woman not much older than myself was standing there. I let her in and wondered what to do next. I got out my Portuguese dictionary and tried my few words in Portuguese like "*boa noite*" ("good evening"). She smiled and said not to worry, or words to that effect. At first I would not touch anything if I could not say the word in Portuguese, and some words were not in the dictionary. The experiment came to a disastrous end in the shower and I was initiated into the wonderful world of Brazilian sex.

Settling In

Since I had arrived at the beginning of the Brazilian summer, classes would not begin for four months. I felt this was more than enough time for me to learn more Portuguese. I did not, however, need Portuguese when I went to one of my first dinners.

Dr. Stephen Wise of New York City had given me a letter of introduction to Dr. Ludwig Lorch, a wealthy German doctor who had fled Nazi Germany. The Lorches lived in a mansion and were one of the wealthiest families in Brazil. His wife was a Klabin, another extremely wealthy Brazilian family. They invited me to dinner and I was awestruck by both the many courses and the number of servants. I met his son, and since he and everyone else spoke perfect English we all had a good time.

I moved quite frequently during my first few months in São Paulo. At the Lorch's suggestion, I first moved to a room over a garage at a boarding house at 68 Rua Nestor Pestani. The best that could be said for the place was its central location: it was near São Paulo's new library and within walking distance of the center of town. My second move was to an English boarding house where I could get some decent food.

Later on I moved in with a Brazilian family on a street called Alemeda Tiete. It was a bungalow with a garden and reminded me of the U.S.A. The family was wonderful - three kids and a dog named Popcorn.

São Paulo seemed like an overgrown small town. I had a shy girlfriend who would bike over to where I was living. We would have long conversations from my bedroom window which was at street level. Of course she never came in despite my repeated invitations.

I always worried about the Rua Augusta *bonde* streetcars (named because the city of São Paulo had issued bonds to pay for the streetcars). Streetcars did not run after eleven o'clock at night, which meant that you had to have your last drink and any other business you were engaged in before that hour. And then there were the elevators; if you wanted to ride an elevator in downtown São Paulo in the early 1940s, you had to have a jacket on or the elevator man would not allow you to pass. You might be without shoes but you had to have a jacket or else you had to use the service elevator.

Social life revolved around the Instituto Brasil-Estados Unidos, a bi-national center that the American government had set up for teaching English to Brazilians. It also pumped out pro-American propaganda and supplied work for the many Americans who were at lose ends and needed some extra cash. John Culver was the dynamic head of the Institute. We often partied together, along with Dona Noemi Silveira Rudolpher (a leading psychiatrist in Brazil), her beautiful niece, George Coleman (the Consul at the U.S. embassy), Benjamin Woodbridge (a professor at the União Cultural Brasil-Estados Unidos), Alexandre Kafka (another professor), John Weir, and Barbara Hadley (a historian of abolitionism).

In general my relations with the American consulate were not good. I think they thought I was a communist because I received the New York newspaper *PM* and *The Nation* magazine. Cecil M. P. Cross was the consul general and a legendary figure who had been there since time immemorial.

In front of the German Consulate was the biggest swastika I had ever seen in my life. I was told by some official at the American Consulate not to take pictures of Swastikas, but how could I resist. I got out my camera and began taking few photos. Suddenly I was tapped on the shoulder by a plain clothes policeman and I was in the hands of the dreaded secret police, the Red Caps of the Vargas dictatorship. The secret police were notorious for their disregard for human rights. I was scared. They put me in a car and took me down to headquarters.

They began to ask me why I was taking photos of the German Consulate. I explained that I did not know it was the German Consulate but there was a swastika and I wanted a photo of a swastika. A likely story! They demanded to know who I was working for and took the film from my camera. As I had seen all the movies about getting into trouble in foreign countries, I demanded the right to phone the American authorities. They responded by taking my passport away from me and now I felt a chill. Without my American passport, which had a certain mysterious power, I was lost. I had seen all the movies where you demanded to see the ambassador. No answer, and as the afternoon passed, no lunch. Now things looked serious. The fact that I hadn't been given lunch was indeed an ominous sign and they kept questioning me.

Apparently they did call the American Consulate and were told that I was a student, but that they had warned me against taking any photos. Wanting to avoid further incidents with Germany, they told the police to "Scare the hell out of him," which they sure did. At the end of the afternoon they gave me my passport back and released me but made me sign a paper that I had not been tortured or injured. I took no more photos of German Swastikas.

Pearl Harbor

The afternoon of Sunday, December 7, 1941 was uneventful. I managed to take my meals at a European *pensão* (boarding house) where I did not learn any Portuguese as everyone spoke English but the food was sure good. After lunch I wandered down to Rua São José, at that time the main street of São Paulo, and saw a startling headline posted on a bulletin board: "*Os Japoneses Atacaram Pearl Harbor.*" I stood there scratching my head and wondering about the headline. "*Os japoneses*" was easy and the word Pearl Harbor was simple too, but that damn word "*atacaram*"? Was it past tense, was it future tense, or was it present tense? I was completely baffled.

There were not many people staring at the poster and I decided to go back to the boarding house and ask some of the old

Brazilians, including a guy who worked at the Consulate, what it was all about. They shook their heads and could not figure out from my Portuguese what the word *atacaron* meant. So we all went down to see the announcement. The trouble was by that time the afternoon soccer scores had begun to arrive and wiped out the news of the attack. There was nothing there.

You could see the lack of importance Brazil gave to that news story. People just didn't put the attack on Pearl Harbor on the top of their list of things to be interested in. A soccer game was much more immediate. The guys kidded me about the announcement and we all returned to the *pensão*.

The radio later that evening confirmed the news. I went to the American Consulate the following day, but they were not very helpful; following our entry into the war the chaos among the diplomats was monumental. I said that I would like to get back to the U.S.A. to join the war, but that I did not have a return ticket. They told me that I was non-essential to the war effort and that I should go to the university, where I would hear from the Consulate if anything changed. Other than picking up my mail there was very little they said to me and or me to them.

I was stranded in Brazil with nothing to do but finish college, so I did. Classes didn't start until March (the end of their summer vacation), so I had some time to learn Portuguese and get to know São Paulo.

Chapter 2: Settling into São Paulo (Winter 1941-42)

In São Paulo, I realized that I was living in a country that was governed as a dictatorship. The dictator was a smiling man with a cigar by the name of Getúlio Vargas[2]. This was most certainly an odd dictatorship; to me, the word "dictator" conjured up the names of Hitler and Mussolini and I was prepared to hate Vargas. I was wrong.

What did it mean to live in and under and around a dictatorship? As a North American I was never even vaguely aware that this was a repressive form of government. I listened to the radio, but my Portuguese was so limited that I had no idea if anything was censored. I had just turned twenty-one and the niceties of civil liberties must have escaped me. My civil liberties were never curtailed, which had to do in part with my nationality. At that time, an American abroad in Latin America could travel almost untouched by the local government.

Over time I became aware that Brazilians did not go about in fear of their lives. There were neither ugly knocks on the door at 2 a.m. nor the disappearance of citizens. The press constantly criticized the Vargas regime, who would then put censors in the offices of the offending newspapers, but after a few months the censor would leave and the cycle would start all over again.

---

[2] Getúlio Dornelles Vargas served as President of Brazil, first as dictator, from 1930 to 1945, and in a democratically elected term from 1951 until his suicide in 1954. He favored nationalism, industrialization, centralization, and social welfare. Though a staunch anti-communist, he was a populist and won the nickname "O Pai dos Pobres" ("The Father of the Poor"). I later authored a book about Vargas and the 1930 Revolution.

However, the government controlled travel, and I had to get a pass to travel deep in the interior. It was issued by the DIP (Department of News and Propaganda), an agency created by the Vargas dictatorship to control the media. To take photographs in the interior I would also have to get permission from the DIP. Though it was a rather ineffectual agency of the government, it did enable the dictatorship to keep tabs on anyone who traveled. Fundamentally, however, people were left alone.

In my letters home I was cautious not to criticize the dictatorship as my mail could possibly be opened. Occasionally I would receive a letter that was cut in half. Professors in my class at the University of São Paulo would make fun of the dictatorship and once in a while a suspicious-looking individual would appear in the classroom. The students quickly told me that he was a police informer.

The easy-going Brazilians did not learn the lesson of what it really was like to live under complete military rule under Vargas. During the 1940's it seemed that he personally ran everything and the army backed him up, and while this backing was sometimes lukewarm and sometimes wholehearted, there wasn't a constant army presence in the streets of Brazil. For these reasons, the later 1964 military coup d'état, one which the middle class and the Paulistas (people from the city of São Paulo) especially supported, was a total surprise to Brazilians. Then they learned about repression; the disappearances, torture, and censorship so common in a dictatorship came about under the military government of the 70's and 80's, not the Vargas regime. Compared to what would occur in the coming decades, Getúlio Vargas was hardly what one would consider totalitarian. It's funny how Brazilians always called him "Getúlio;" when you called someone by their first name it was almost affectionate and friendly.

One famous feature of the Vargas period was the "*Hora do Brasil*," when the government took over the airwaves; it was called the hour of silence as everyone turned off their radios - at least in the cities. But in the interior of the country it was a different question. The radio was the only way the government could communicate directly with the people. There was one radio in a small town and it was located in the central square of the town. People gathered at night to hear the government news and any other news that Vargas thought they should hear.

During the lull before the university started I met a strange and wonderful man by the name of Paul Vanorden Shaw. A. Ph.D. from Columbia University and a newspaper reporter, he suggested that as part of my education concerning Brazil, I should join him in attending the Third Inter American Conference of Foreign Ministers. This was being held in January 1942 in Rio de Janeiro, so off I went.

The Third Inter American Conference of Foreign Ministers

The meeting of the Foreign Ministers of Latin America had been convened at the request of the United States in the hopes of obtaining a unanimous declaration of war against the Germans and Japanese. I described it in a letter home:

January 16, 1942

Dear Folks;

The first and combined session met yesterday and boy it was a killer. The first session was where all the principal delegates made their speeches and it looks like it is the U.S. all the way. Later on this week I may be able to attend some of the closed sessions. I did meet President Roosevelt's cousin but I was remarkably unimpressed.

There is a different spirit here in Rio. Things that are worthy of comment in São Paulo are not true in Rio. Here the press are beating the drums for war while every editorial you read in São Paulo is always one that cautions the readers because Brazil has nothing to gain by getting into this war and Brazil cannot aid the USA.

Yesterday when the Ministers were making their speeches I went down to the Avenida Rio Branco and stopped by the taxis stands to listen to the speeches and watch the reactions of the people. The speech that seemed to invoke a lot of enthusiasm though I have not read it yet was by the Chilean Ambassador who opened the meeting. While he was speaking the people around the cab kept saying "Formidavel" and good and those are my sentiments too.

Later on the evening the Mexican Ambassador spoke and it seems he almost came out for a declaration of war against Germany and received an ovation that almost brought the house down.

I am more than a little worried about this outward support. I feel a lot of it may fall through because when these men meet in small sessions we are going to see what they can get out of Uncle Sam. For all their good words in the way of money it comes from the USA for factories and developing their industries. I am overly pessimistic and I can't help but keep my fingers crossed. I don't know what power these men at the conference have. But I don't think that it is too much.

I am going to the beach now. I will write later. I am staying on Copacabana Beach at a Pensão where I pay 75 cents a day with another American student for room and board. He is financing me until I get some money so I am not complaining.

Met Pedro Calmon, one of Brazil's greatest historians, and I hope to do some work with him when I return to São Paulo.

Love, Jordan

My diary notes continue about the same events.

Sumner Welles and a most serious young reporter (top left of photo). From the *O Cruzeiro* article.

> The Foreign Ministers of Latin America and the USA met in Rio on January 15, 1942, six weeks after the attack on Pearl Harbor. The United States was determined to get a united declaration of war from her Latin American allies against the Axis powers. We were going to try and get all the Latin American nations to show their solidarity with the USA in a war declaration against Germany. The United States sent Undersecretary of State Sumner Welles to do the job.
>
> Bad mistake.
>
> His style and character seemed to be everything the Brazilians detested. No warmth and charisma ever appeared. Impeccably dressed and cold and detached, he seemed to be doing a job he detested.
>
> Brazil vacillated between being pro Axis and pro Allies, but by the time the Conference began Vargas had shifted his position to be slightly pro American. There was however a good deal of fascist sentiment around. At the conference, the man who saved the USA position was Dr. Osvaldo Aranha, the charismatic Brazilian who had been a former Ambassador to the USA and Getúlio Vargas's Minister of Foreign Relations. He was frankly and openly pro-American. He presided over the meetings and was the only prominent Brazilian who openly favored the Allies and the United States.

(I was to become better acquainted with Dr. Aranha in 1949 when I returned to Brazil with my masters thesis on the 1930 Revolution that brought Vargas to power. But that is later history.)

Aranha and Vargas had already signed the accord that would permit Brazilian territory to be used by American forces as bases against the Axis. This alone was a startling fact as the Brazilians had been badly treated by the British in the previous century and were extremely sensitive concerning territorial integrity. After a lot of talk, Brazil broke off diplomatic relations with Germany. The Argentine delegation would not even consider this position, while the Mexican Ambassador electrified the audience with his fiery speeches in favor of the Americans. Many of these meetings were held in the old Palácio Tiradentes, where the Municipal Council of Rio meets today.

Other meetings were held in the old Palácio do Itamaraty, the location of the Brazilian State Department. This was a group of buildings from the Imperial period, with columns and a reflecting pool in which swans floated gracefully. Security was nonexistent and the fact that I spoke English and looked American was enough to get me past the security guards. I got into private meetings with my old high school press pass. It made no bones about it, saying "De Witt Clinton High School Press." It worked though, and I used it to admit me to the proceedings. Why I still had it after two years of college I will never know.

O Cruzeiro, a national news magazine, carried a photo of Sumner Welles[3] and me and a few others. I was pretending to be a reporter with my pad of paper and furiously taking notes while not understanding a word of what was going on. Clearly this was a laid-back country where anything was possible.

While I was in Rio attending the Inter American Conference, I dropped into the office of *TIME* Magazine and met Jane Braga, *TIME*'s reporter for Brazil. She looked like a tough female reporter from out of the movies. I also met a young lady who came into office searching for her lost panties, which had been left on the desk the night before after a rather wild party in the office. I liked this atmosphere-it fit in with my ideas of Brazil and newspaper reporting.

Waiting for Classes to Start

After the conference, I returned to São Paulo and waited for classes to start in March (fall in Brazil). My letters home were full of events around me as well as some angst as to what to do with my life before the university started:

February 5, 1942

Dear Folks,

It is just 4:30 now and I know because the German VASP airline plane just flew over heading for Rio and at the same time served the purpose of reminding me that on this birthday that I write to you I am not in my usual place and the world is not in its usual state. I think Dad that if people on their birthdays wrote down a summary of the events they would have a history book that would be great Let the person record what happened on their birthday they would have their own private summary of world history Well the last time I was in Illinois this time in

---

[3] Sumner Welles was Under-Secretary of State from 1937-43 under President Franklin D. Roosevelt. Wealthy, elegant, and well-connected, he had also been Assistant Secretary of State for Latin American Affairs. He was forced to resign in 1943 for personal reasons. Winston Churchill said of him, "I think 'no comment' is a splendid expression; I got it from Sumner Welles."

Brazil – let's hope that next birthday letter to you will find me closer to home.

Your loving son, Jordan

February 10, 1942

Dear Folks,

Time magazine came through. This is only in the subscription department but they asked me to find out a few things for them. In the mean time they are sending me TIME air express which costs $10.00. But I went further than they asked. Not only did I answer the questions they asked but I made a thorough investigation into the dealer who was handling TIME here. I finally made my five page report and uncovered more dirt than the city dump holds. Might be a job here. They could use a person like me and I did not hesitate to tell them so.

Love, Jordan

Feb 13, 1942

Dear Folks,

What the devil did I write in my letter of January 26th? First off your sentence was sliced off and all that was left was that you had heard it on the radio. Now that seems damned silly if you can hear anything the radio that is censorable we could if, we wanted to, catch it on short wave. It seems to have been the USA censors not the British. But I am not sure and I wish you would check because there are people here who are interested in knowing what this is all about.

I am living for the present in a boarding house but I can place a good bet that I will not be here next month. I am really putting pressure on for a home and I think one will show up a the end of the month.

Love, Jordan

February 24 1942

Dear Folks,

I am in a quandary. A real honest to goodness quandary. Not the garden variety type but the real home grown type that must be solved by yourself type of quandary. It may all be a tempest in teapot but I will outline to you a few of the details. I have a chance for work at the American Consulate. I spoke to the Consul-General and told him that I wanted to be of any assistance I could around the office. He sent me to his assistant who was busy and I must seem him tomorrow. If I get a job here it will be a $100 and month and $40 for maintenance. Oh gosh I don't know what to do. I don't think I can take any school courses if I take this job. I do not know which opens up more future. I can take two courses at night school here. But at the moment I am going along as if nothing happened and tomorrow after I see the man I will put a post script in this letter if anything happened. So much for my troubles: may they always be this vein.

I got the TIME magazine subscription because of the report I made for them. We heard President Roosevelt's speech here last night and it felt good to hear his voice down here.

I am moving Saturday into a pensão that is mostly inhabited by English people but at least I will get food that I can eat. At my present place all I got was an orange and, when they had it, three slices of dry bread and butter and a glass of half water and half milk which I could not drink. At the new place we can get bacon, eggs and jam and orange juice. Also I could not get a desk lamp and I will have one in the new place.

My stay in Rio de Janeiro cost me plenty and the boarding house lady did not take off hardly anything when I left. But I am paying off the debt by the money I get from teaching English to some student.

Dr. Lorch helped me to get to the Rio Conference by introducing me to someone who was very interesting [Dr. Paul Vanorden Shaw]. He got me into the Conference. My fare to Rio de Janeiro on the train was almost six dollars which is nothing to sneeze at. Yes the dancers (Kay Katya and Kay) were really great to me. As I told you I was their guest again during the Christmas and New Years holidays at the swankiest hotel in Santos.

Concerning the registration fees at the university. Well the Escola Livre starts about the 12th of March with the tuition about 550 mil reis which is about 30 dollars with an extra 5 dollars for the Portuguese exam. I may be able to take courses at the Universidade de São Paulo, where the cost is six or seven dollars. They start in the middle of March.

I got up at 7:30 had coffee and went downtown to União Cultural Brasil-Estados Unidos and took a Portuguese lesson from 9:30 to 10:30 then went to the consulate for my mail. Next to a pupil I have who I am teaching English to. She is a radio singer from whom I get a few dollars a week . That lasts until 12. Then walk home to lunch and finish at 1:15. I study or read until 1:45 when I have another pupil from 2 till 4 and then back to the Consulate and home to study until supper at seven. It is hard for me to study at night as I have a single 60 watt bulb hanging down from the ceiling which is very bad for my eyes. The parcel as has not come yet and a number of ships have been sunk.

I wonder if I will ever get out of here. I am paying the same at the new place but I am sharing a room with this fellow I went to Rio with. As I told you in the last letter the TIME magazine job possibility is progressing very well and there is a chance of a job.

Love, Jordan

March 3, 1942

Dear Folks,

Two very nice things happened this week. First I moved. I live in a different part of town and I am sharing a room with another boy who is working at the American Consulate. We are living in a *pensão* or boarding house and have two huge rooms[4]. One of which we use for sleeping and the other we made into a living room. I am paying the same but he is paying the extra cost of the place. I pay 20 dollars a month and he pays 25.

It is more or less an English place but two of the English people that live here also teach Portuguese and English so I get an hour or two from them. The food compared to the other place is just wonderful. I get fruit with cereal, a soft boiled egg, two glasses of real milk, and breakfast jam. As a result my health is picking up. I have lost a bit of weight but now everything will straighten itself out.

Second thing I wanted to mention was the fact that I received your February 21st letter with the 25 dollars in it. And the extra 5 dollars needless to say hit the spot. I paid off my rent today and I will be having a stable time for a while.

I went around to all my schools to begin checking up on when and what to expect and have the following to report. The Escola Livre should start the 12th and the U of São Paulo starts the 16th or 17th of March. But I will need 10 dollars for the U of São Paulo. I feel that all the good that I did at the University of Illinois is becoming undone. But give me another month and I will be back in there pitching.

If this TIME job clicks then my financial worries will be all over. I am eagerly awaiting a reply to my last letter. I believe I told you that they were sending me a subscription to the airmail edition of TIME. I am sorry that my last article was so bad but I never claimed to be a writer and if I should write anything it is secondary to the fact that I want to be

---

[4] I shared this apartment with a man from California named Paul Oechsli who was there on a Rotary fellowship. I will always have a sort spot in my heart for the Rotary, because later on, Paul's checks supported not only him but me, when my check didn't come from the U.S.A.

a history professor5. Perhaps I am rationalizing. I would appreciate it if when something is lousy you say so rather than not. I am working with other stuff but I am resolved not to send something foul and waste postage stamps.

About the parcel it hasn't arrived yet and I have my fears as all those ships have been sunk. Was there any explanation of your censored letter? Anything you remember that was worthwhile repeating because most of your letters have not been censored at all. Your remark about beautiful daughters waiting to be palmed off. There isn't any such animal down here. I haven't seen anyone here yet that I would like to hold a conversation with at breakfast and don't think I will.

Love, Jordan

March 10, 1942

Dear Folks,

Received your last letter in 5 days. You sent it out the 2nd of March and I got it the 5th. It shows you how mail can be handled when the censors do not mess around with it.

I and a group of Americans heard Roosevelt's speech down here on shortwave. I managed to go to someone's house with a shortwave radio and we get news from the States which is pretty fresh yet. I still like your clippings better. I don't know why but I was not particularly effected by the President's speech. I guess I get the impression that actions are needed not words. I often hesitate to make any statements about world politics because I am very detached here.

We heard that another Brazilian ship was torpedoed but it produced little stir.

I am in an almost homelike atmosphere here. There are only three people here beside me and my roommate. Three of them are young English girls who were born Brazilians and you would get a kick out of hearing them start a sentence in English and ending in Portuguese. Sometimes it sounds like Chinese they switch so much. The food is wonderfully clean and wholesome with fresh lettuce and tomato salad at every meal. There is an old lady who serves the table and scolds us when we don't eat the fresh vegetables. I feel right at home.

Jeepers Creepers here I am typing along and I forgot to tell you that I took my Portuguese exam this morning and I think I passed it O.K. Golly you people will never know what a thrill it is to start a conversation in

---

[5] I was thinking of becoming a history professor as early as 1942 and I succeeded in 1956. - JMY March 7, 2005

Portuguese and carry on without stopping to think in English. Yes about the teacher part of that offer at the American Graded School here, I delivered a short speech to the high school class describing the Rio Conference and the principal of the school, a Miss Moore, asked me if I would like to teach the Current Events course twice a week. I don't know yet. I have to see how the classes at my school work out .You know it will be good experience for me.

Hey about that parcel you sent I have not seen hide nor hair of it yet. I hope it is not at the bottom of the South Atlantic.

Listen I might as well let you know about the financial side of my trip to Rio. First of all after much cussing and howling the landlady as I told you did not take off more than what amounted to three dollars so you could actually say that she did not take off anything. Second it cost about 25 bucks in Rio and the ten you sent me for carfare .But I had a streak of luck that has ended unfortunately. I was able to pay off of my roommate with the money I made from a student I had last month. She is a radio actor who is going to the US and wants someone to teach her conversational English for which she gave me $15.00.

Love, Jordan

Finally March arrived and classes at the Universidade de São Paulo began.

Chapter 3. The First Semester in Brazil (Spring 1942)

Classes turned out to be fun, but I'd been a poor student at the University of Illinois and I was a poor student at University of São Paulo. Traveling 10,000 miles did not improve my powers of concentration.

The branch of the university I was attending was located in the Praça da República in downtown São Paulo. It was an impressive building built in the Belle Epoch style. The steps leading up the building were wide and spacious, and the classrooms were huge, with tall windows that opened on to the square. The first two floors belonged to the normal school and the third floor was the university's Faculty of History and Geography. It was an impressive building, built as the Paulistas imagined Parisians would have done.

The warmth and friendliness of my fellow students impressed me. Students were fascinated with me. Here was a *Norte Americano* and of course everyone took turns practicing their English on me and I reciprocated by getting Portuguese lessons out of them. They knew all sorts of things about the U.S.A. and they expected me to know what they didn't, such as how many Puerto Ricans were in the U.S.A., how many blacks there were in New York City, and if the subway system there had been built by slaves. I promptly bombed out but I knew that slaves had not built the subways in New York City. They seemed to know everything about contemporary life in the U.S.A., like the crime rate in the major American cities and the pregnancy rate among teenagers. They knew what was going on in the U.S.A. because they had seen it in the movies. The cinema was the U.S.A.

I bought myself a notebook and began my studies. I inscribed in the cover: "It is not I that belong to the past, but the past that belongs to me" The quote came from *The Epic of America*[6] and I thought it sounded cool. It sounds funny in this age, when everyone is pursuing their roots.

My fellow students assumed I was a fugitive from the war and that I had fled from the U.S.A. to avoid the draft. I tried to explain that I was registered with the Embassy and if any transportation showed up I would take the first boat back, but to no avail. I also had no doubt that the U.S.A. would win the war and said so in no uncertain terms. That baffled the students, who saw the U.S.A. and the Allied forces losing all over the world. The year 1942 was a bad one for the United States, but I continued to be optimistic.

The small café across the Praça da República provided me with my breakfast; a *coxinha de galinha* (a chicken leg surrounded by mashed potatoes) and a *cafezinho* (a tiny cup of black coffee). The Rua Barão de Itapeninga, which ran into the Praça da República, was a sophisticated shopping street; I would amble along it on my way to the university. It was full of expensive jewelry stores, fashion shops, and mouth-watering goodies in costly tea shops along the way.

At the *Faculdade de Ciências e Letras*[7], I took two courses: “The History of Brazil” and “Brazilian Geography.”

The Brazilian History Course

The Brazilian history course was taught by Prof. Alfredo Ellis Jr., who turned out to be fascinating[8]. A fierce Paulista, he regaled the class with stories about São Paulo’s resistance to the Vargas dictatorship. Glass marbles were thrown from his classroom window into the streets to stop the mounted police from arresting

---

6 *The Epic of America* was a history of the United States written by James Truslow Adams in 1933. In it, he coined the phrase “the American dream.”

7 Brazilian universities, like those in Europe, are organized into “faculties” (*faculdades*) which are like groups of departments in a university in the U.S.A. Faculties operate more independently than departments do in the U.S.A. Students don’t apply to the university for admission, they apply to the particular faculty in which they want to study.

8 Prof. Alberto Ellis, Jr. graduated from the Faculty of Law at the University of São Paulo in 1917. He was a São Paulo state senator from 1925-30 and 1934-37 and fought in the Revolution of 1932. He joined the faculty of USP in 1941.

student protesters. Unfortunately for me he lisped and to this day I say certain words in Portuguese that I learned in his class with a lisp. He also went out of his way to shock my perceptions of American history, explaining the licentious parts of early Puritan life to a Norte Americano as I had never heard it before.

Professor Ellis thought it would be an interesting idea if I did a research paper on the Americans who had immigrated to Brazil after the Civil War. (Several groups of Confederates had fled to Brazil after the South lost the Civil War; others had emigrated to Mexico). I was considered a Yankee by the Brazilians and everyone thought it would be fun if I went down and interviewed these Southern descendants of the remaining settlers. I was amazed to find the remnants of the Civil War Americans who had founded a town called Vila Americana.

There were three such immigrant colonies set up in Brazil. One was at Santarém in the state of Pará in the Amazon; one on the River Doce in the state of Espirito Santo; and the last at Santa Barbara in São Paulo where I was at that time. At Santa Barbara the families fanned out to the nearby districts of Bom Retiro, Campo Station, and Vila Americana. In 1942, there were 35 families who still considered themselves Americans. The strangeness of their customs, religion, and language had initially kept them apart from the Brazilians, but as the years wore on they married among themselves and then later intermarried with Brazilians. They had a school with English teachers up until 1925. One of the teachers was Mr. Joel Sanders, a southerner from Troy, Alabama who taught there until 1900.

They had two Protestant churches and the only thing they had in common - according to the man I interviewed - was their distaste for the Catholic Church. Since the Catholics would not let the Protestants be buried in their cemeteries, the little town had two separate cemeteries, and most of the people buried in their cemetery were Confederate veterans. Basket parties and fish fries were celebrated in annual parties up until 1930. One old timer told me that the last really big one was in 1911 before World War I broke out.

They offered me southern cooking - some weird bread that they called corn pone and southern fried chicken - which I could hardly stomach. I made a list of all the descendants who were there. Their accents were not southern.

A procession of actors at the *congada* of Ilhabela.

Many descendants were of mixed race, though I was amused by one story that mentioned a man who had gone native and married a Black (which, to a community of expatriated Confederates, was quite the scandal). Another concerned the "Sweet Millers" who had gone to the Rio Doce area. The word *doce* translates as sweet and they were in contrast to the "Bitter Millers" who settled there in Vila Americana. I later dated one of the girl descendants, named Belita Pyles.

Later on in 1943, when I was working up the Amazon River, I ran into the descendants of another group of Civil War refugees with the family name of Riker. The original Riker claimed he had been carried down in his mother's arms. Eighty years old when I met him in 1943, he had about 20 illegitimate kids running around the town of Santarém with a wide range of skin colors[9].

The Geography Course

The second course I took was one taught by Prof. Aroldo de Azevedo, called "The Geography of Brazil." Prof. Azevedo was the author of many textbooks on Brazilian geography. That was a no-nonsense course. He ran a tight ship and was very authoritarian.

My Portuguese was so bad that for the first few months I barely understood what was going on. When the class laughed, I laughed. When the class wrote, I wrote like a madman, not understanding a word of what was being said.

Prof. Azevedo took us on field trips to such places as Caraguatatuba (a city on the shore of northern São Paulo state) and

[9] The Riker family arrived in Santarém in 1867, headed by Robert Henry Riker, who had run an iron works in Charleston, South Carolina. He and his wife and five children settled along the Rio Tapajos in the town of Diamantino and turned to agriculture and rubber production. They were among the first in Brazil to plant groves of rubber trees for harvesting latex. Jordan probably met Robert's son David Bowman Riker.

Ilhabela. Ilhabela was memorable for the "*congada*[10]" that the local residents played out for us, a story of the *Mouros* versus the *Cristões* (Moors vs. Christians). These folklore legends were carried over from Portugal and were still being dramatized on a tropical island off the coast of Brazil in the South Atlantic. Men lined up with swords and lances on one side; facing them on the other side were the Moors. The *Cristões* always won the battles.

One memorable night we stayed in a Catholic monastery sharing their food and prayers. We students solemnly sat at a long table trying to appear seriously pious. As it turns out we may have been the most pious people there that night; it was common knowledge, the students informed me, that the housekeepers and cooks were sexual companions of the priests.

On another bus trip we stopped at Mogi da Cruzes and other towns in the Paraíba Valley that runs from the city of São Paulo into the state of Rio de Janeiro. It was as a result of these trips that I began to sense the complexity of Brazil. I got a feel for the sweep, grandeur, and contour of the country and was awed by the vast areas that were not productive and yet had such potential.

On one geographical field trip sex reared its ugly head one Friday when night all the guys decided to go the local red light district. We were in a small town in the interior of São Paulo and the red light district was pretty poor. I was invited to go but pleaded

The Geography class of 1942 of the University of São Paolo. A surprising number of women took the course, for the time. I am in the back row on the right.

that I had a headache, though in reality I couldn't handle this sort of thing. I kept explaining that we did not pay for this in the United States. They asked me who the devil we did it with. Did we use "family" girls? I was baffled. All girls come from families; what other kind of girls were there? Then I remembered a dance I went to when I was studying in São Paulo. The dances all started terribly late, at about 11 o'clock. Later that evening I said to the girl I was dancing with, "Why don't we go into the garden and cool off?" (I thought it would be fun to smooch a bit, but nothing doing). The chaperon at the door had explained that these were "family" girls.

Professor Azevedo took his material very seriously. I have the proofs of an exam I took in which he attempted to correct my Portuguese but gave up after three pages. I was attempting to compare the state of Rio Grande do Sul to the state of Illinois. There's no comparison: Rio Grande was Brazil's most southern state, a producer of wine and leather goods, and as far I was concerned Illinois just produced corn.

The Escola Livre

The other school at I enrolled in, the Escola Livre de Sociologia e Política de São Paulo (Free School of Sociology and Politics), gave me an entirely different experience. This was the school that had sent the catalog that caught my eye to the University of Illinois.

A Brazilian by the name of Dr. Cyro Berlinck was a prime force behind its existence. He had pulled together a strange group of scholars from the University of Chicago and some refugee professors from Europe who had fled the Nazis. Alexandre Kafka, a young economics instructor from Czechoslovakia, went on to become executive director of the International Monetary Fund (1966-1998). The American faculty had all studied and taken degrees under Talcott Parsons, a professor of sociology at Harvard. They were teaching sociology in the style of the University of Chicago and they were trail-blazers. Their impact on the Brazilian educational system is impressive; most of the commonly-held views of race and class in modern Brazil are a result of their work.

To me, Dr. Donald Pierson was the most surprising professor. A Midwesterner from the University of Chicago, his classes were quite popular but the students implored him to speak English instead of the mangled Portuguese in which he delivered his lectures. Strangely, I understood his Portuguese perfectly.

Dr. Pierson had written a pioneering book analyzing the Black community in Bahia. He pointed out that blacks and whites in the lower income groups tended to intermarry while those in upper income groups did not - a reverse of what went on in the U.S.A. His research indicated that you got the same damned awful low wage in Bahia regardless of your skin color, so there was there was no advantage to marrying into white groups for improved status.

He also insisted that there was a distinct mixed group of people who were mulattoes and thus did not fall into the white or black classification. What he was saying was that Brazil did have a definite population of mixed-race or mulatto people. In the United States we were taught that one was either black or white - nothing in between - and that lower income Americans have the greatest prejudice while in Brazil it was the very rich whites who feared or disliked blacks.

The role of the Catholic Church was important in that it approved marriage between Indians and Portuguese. The lack of Portuguese women was significant in the colonial period, and thus the church began to approve multi-racial marriages. Black ambition faced no legal opposition; in Brazil a black man can achieve middle class status if he wishes to strive and accomplish. There are some cautions to this analysis. We had to read heavily in Robert E. Park and Ernest Burgess, but most of this went over my head, and of course we read Gilberto Freyre's *The Masters and the Slaves*[11], which I assimilated easily.

Once they brought in Prof. Alfred Radcliffe-Brown, a world renowned lecturer from Oxford. I listened politely to his lectures but had no idea who he was and where he was coming from. At the time, he was one of the most famous anthropologists in the world. He had studied southeast Polynesia, including the Andaman Islands and Tonga. The Brazilian students fell all over him but I thought he was a jerk.

The other class that fascinated me was the course given by Dr. Herbert Baldus, a German refugee, on the Brazilian Indians. He

---

[11] *The Masters and the Slaves* (*Casa Grande e Senzala*) was a sociological treatise on race relations written in 1933. In it, Freyre described the patriarchal system of the "Big House" and the slave dwelling, and argued in favor of the mixing of races.

lectured to us about Kurt Nimuendajú, a German-Brazilian ethnologist who had gone to live with the Indians. We engaged in a thorough study on the Tapirapé Indians who lived in the south of the state of Pará (now Tocantins), on the Island of Bananal. For some reason or other the description of the pristine waters of the Araguaia River impressed me and the lives of the Indians there as described by Dr. Baldus were mesmerizing. Sixty years later I still have a clear image of the island.

Letters Home

As excerpts from the following letters indicate, I learned about Brazil in many ways:

April 1, 1942

Dear Folks,

I have just received a taste of Brazilian schools. Holidays have just been declared at the University of São Paulo from this Tuesday until next Monday. So we students have to cool our heels after the first week of school. Thank goodness the Escola Livre does not close up until Wednesday or Thursday, I hope.

I don't think I will go anywhere for Easter. Perhaps as it only costs a dollar I'll go down to São Vicente. This is the oldest town in Brazil founded 1502 or 1512. It seems the historians have not yet decided and it seems a really interesting place close to the port city of Santos..

Oh yes. There was a German caught here in São Paulo with a terrifically powerful short wave radio which sent information constantly to Germany. He seemed to be an important guy and everyone was greatly relieved when he was put in jail and his equipment confiscated.

Love, Jordan

April 12, 1942

Dear Folks,

Well today I feel I accomplished something. I spent the whole day studying and turned down all sorts of invitations to go boating and on picnics.

Your package arrived. It is at the Post Office. I received a notice that I should come down to the Central Office as there was a package for me. But there is a catch. No one in São Paulo has ever succeeded in getting a package out of the Post Office for less than 5 weeks. It is agonizing to know that it is so near and yet so far. But eventually you will get it out. You see they measure and inspect everything. They measure stocking lengths, they take down the brand numbers and they test the quality of the cloth and they register every article on about 12 different forms that have to be filled out separately for a variety of different agencies. So I have hopes of getting it this month. (This was the law of similarities at work. It was to make sure you did not import things that were made in Brazil.)

There is a vague chance that I may have the opportunity to go up into Indian country for my vacation. This is way up into the state of Mato Grosso where few white men have been. A group of fellows may go up in an expedition to study the Indians and I'm trying to go. You know I bought a huge map of Brazil that I have hung in front of my desk and when you look at it you see how much of this continent has not even been opened up. Just the sea coast has been touched by the Brazilians. You must realize that there are only capitals of six states that have been reached by railroads and that was only to get produce out. Now they are reached by plane or by trucks and very bad roads

Love, Jordan

When my first semester ended, there was a break before the fall semester began, and I decided to explore Brazil outside São Paulo.

Chapter 4. Summer Interlude (June-July 1942)

Summer in America is the Brazilian winter. During this time, I took several breaks from classes to explore the vastness of the country and wrote extensively in my diary. As my writings show, I also fretted over not being able to go back to the U.S.A.

The first two trips - to Dedo de Deus and Espirito Santo – were made with Robert Holland, an Englishman born in Brazil. Robert was actually a second generation Brazilian and it was odd to hear him say later that I was the first poor American he had met in Brazil. All the other Americans had been rich members of the country club set. The third trip, to Gomez, was with my São Paulo roommate, Paul Oechsli (he of the wonderful Rotary fellowship).

The Trip to Dedo de Deus

In late June, 1942, Robert Holland and I decided that it would be fun to travel up to the River Doce area, about 350 miles north of Rio de Janeiro, and see what the place looked like. The following diary notes record this trip.

June 25, 1942

Strange as it seems I am in Rio de Janeiro and have been here since Tuesday night the 23rd, when Robert Holland and I took the 7 a.m. Rio de Janeiro train from Sao Paulo's Norte Station. We had met in front of the Caixa Economica [Savings and Loan] building about 6:15 a.m. The weather was terrible – a foggy misty day and the city took a long time coming to life. We arrived in Rio about 8 p.m. that night. The thing that constantly amazes an American about the railroads is the fact that the trains are all wood and the sanitation facilities stink to high heaven. The dining room car was very clean and we bought ham and cheese sandwiches and a Brazilian soft drink called *guaraná*. Again the fact that people wore white linen traveling coats to protect them from the dust and smoke in the tunnels surprised me.

When we arrived we grabbed a cab for Copacabana Beach which cost us 25 mil réis. We slept at the Banhos. [The Banhos were an American family living in Rio and who opened their apartment to every stray American in Brazil.] Had a milk shake and coke at the Lojas Americanas [local department store]. Coke was just being introduced into Brazil. Wednesday we spent on the beach. At night we went to the Atlantico Casino and I gambled for the first time in my life. I lost 50 cents at the roulette wheel.

Met two American aviators who are piloting Flying Fortresses [B-17 airplanes] to Africa.

June 26, 1942

We went to Arpoador, a beach that separates Copacabana from Ipanema and is a huge flat rock at the beginning of the beach. It has some coastal guns located in an underground fortress and while we were sitting on the rocks they decided to fire their off shore guns which almost blew us off the rocks.

Went down town in the afternoon to the Instituto Brasil-Estados Unidos and met Mr. Thomas and Miss Nogais. Later I met with Miss Jane Braga of TIME and LIFE. We might work out something I hope. She mentioned that I might help in a LIFE magazine layout.

Rained like hell all day and we went down town and visited H. S. Polin Laboratories. They are working on turning a lot of the surplus coffee beans into plastic. Really a complete lab. Then we went to the city of Niteroi across the Bay of Guanabara from Rio de Janeiro. This is the capital of the state of Guanabara. We took a ferry boat and it cost 80 Réis. It took almost half day to get there. Visited the Icarai Casino, which was on the beach, and saw a good show for nothing. They have a great system down here. You can see a floor show just by going in and pretending to gamble.

June 27, 1942

Had a breakfast in the Bar Saturnia and there was big picture of Getulio Vargas on the wall. At noon we grabbed our stuff and took the train to Teresópolis. 16 mil réis first class. We jumped off the train at Victor Banho's ranch. It is called Rancho Dedo de Deus and is in the shadow of the mountain. It was strange jumping off the train in the rain. We just estimated that we were close and jumped. We walked to the cabin and built a fire and had supper. Then all three us piled into the same bed and fought over blankets the whole night.

June 28, 1942

Weather cleared up a little; still very cold but nowhere near freezing. The Dedo de Deus (called that because some rocks look like a finger pointed to heaven) came out of the fog. We found some old ruins later on. There was the old Emperor's road[12], which runs near here and was a stopping off station for the Emperor on the trip back to Rio from Teresópolis. The trip in those days was a long and hard one. There was a caved in dungeon on wall with just three window bars sticking above ground. Very spooky with the tangled underbrush all around. I'll bet some scientific investigation would show amazing things.

Later in the day we hiked to Teresópolis and bought food for three days. We said goodbye to Victor, who had to return to Rio. Then through the mist and the fog and darkness we walked back to the Rancho. When we entered a gorge at one point, there was a sharp silhouette of the surrounding mountains. It looked very unreal. It was the night of the full moon. We went to sleep and had a hell of a battle with a mouse. I think the mouse won as I got up every ten minutes to see what time it was.

June 29, 1942

Met the train about 7:15 a.m. and grabbed a bottle of milk from the conductor. The engineer had obligingly slowed the train down (Victor has made arrangements with the train crew so that they delivered a bottle of milk to us every morning). We made breakfast and cleaned house (just a saw a hummingbird) and then we started to build a table. I don't know if we will ever finish it. It is still amazing to me to go out of the house and hack down a tree with a *facão*, which is two sided steel blade about 15 inches long. I am going to bring one home with me. I haven't shaved in about six days.

I made supper–French toast and scrambled eggs and sausages. After supper it cleared up and the stars shown brilliantly. The stars of the Cruzeiro do Sul[13] were exceptionally clear. We put the radio on and it was playing some symphonic music I think it was Pictures from Exhibition I don't know but I do know that standing there under the

---

[12] Named for the last emperor of Brazil, Dom Pedro II. Pedro II is widely considered one of the greatest Brazilians in history and presided over the Empire's "golden age" during the mid-19th century, but was ousted by a military coup in 1889.

[13] The *Cruzeiro do Sul* (Southern Cross), besides being one of the most prominent constellations in the southern hemisphere, has long been a national symbol in Brazil; it was prominently displayed on the seal of the old Empire (1822-1889) and is as well on the flag of the Republic (1889-present)

stars with black crags of the mountains outlined on all four sides made me feel very primitive. Can't explain it but grabbed the big machete and wanted to hit some thing or do something physical - screwy.

June 30, 1942

We tore out to the train and damn if there was no milk on it. We felt very silly standing there waiting for a bottle of milk and no milk came. I whipped up a good supper about 2:30 and did not finish until 5:30. We worked on the table again all morning then got tired and lay down to sleep.

Robert got ill in the late afternoon and he didn't have any supper. He went to sleep as it got dark but I sat outside and watched the moon rise. At night the animals signal to each other. At first you jump but soon get used to it. The wind really howled last night and practically tore off our tin roof. Going home tomorrow – running out of food.

July 1, 1942

Each day we stay out here it gets nicer and nicer and we get more accustomed to it. Missed first two trains in the morning and just managed to catch the third train with milk on it. Robert ran out without his trousers and had to come back.

We spent most of the morning cleaning up because we plan to take the afternoon train to Rio. We had some food left over and we decided to give it to an old woman we met. We packed up after lunch and began hiking. We left our knapsacks at Soberbo [a nearby town] and hiked in to Alto. Had a very expensive lunch and then took a bus to Várzea. Robert got an idea that we should take a buggy ride to the Cascata do Imbuí (a waterfall) which took about two hours and was a heck of a lot of fun.

Caught a train at the Alto and met a pretty blond English girl. We joked about being lost and she befriended us. When we arrived in Rio, she spoke to her father and drove us 'poor lost strangers' out to Copacabana. We had supper and slept at Victor's apartment again.

July 2, 1942

Spent the day in a mad whirl. Had lunch with Sylvio downtown and then went to Instituto where we got in touch with Dr. Pontual who gave us piles of information about Vitória, the capital of state of Espirito Santo.

We plan to leave tomorrow night. Went to Lloyd Brasileiro [a travel agency] but could not get a ship to Vitória. Then went to DIP and they sent a telegram to the Chief of DIP in Vitória that we were coming. What a life! Had supper at Victor [Banho]'s. Then I went to see Three Bananas up stairs. Slept at the Midkiffs' house and am now sitting in a Street Car heading for Copacabana. We just passed Sugar Loaf and the top was covered with clouds. It looked so sad.

Chief of Police was arrested. Brazilian Ship sunk and the students promise to demonstrate tomorrow.

July 3, 1942

I did not want to disturb [Harold] Midkiff; in fact they did not even know that I had slept at their apartment. Had a nice breakfast there and chatted with the maid. Went to the Instituto Brasil-Estados Unidos and met Dr. Melville J. Herskovits[14] and he seems a very nice guy. Lunch at Victor's and then to Jane Braga's office. There was an American girl there with the improbable name of Baby. She had left a pair of woman's panties on the desk and was embarrassedly looking for them.

While I was there Ed Bagley[15] of the Associated Press came in and spoke to Braga. I was in awe as he seemed to create an air of excitement about him as if he was the embodiment of history in the making. I don't know why but whenever I see him I want to work in journalism.

Bagley reported that the Chief of Police of Rio de Janeiro is a fascist sympathizer. Vargas has had him arrested until he resigns, which apparently he won't do. There were some Nazis rounded up by the Chief of Police Müller and nothing came of it. The Interventor of the state of Rio de Janeiro, Amaral Peixoto[16], kidnapped them and took them to Niteroi (the capital of Rio and across the Bay from Rio) and third degreed them into talking.

Tomorrow is the 4th of July and the students are demonstrating against the Axis powers. The students asked the government that they use the Police of the Justice Department rather than those of Chief of Police Müller[17]. It seems that Müller's police will cause trouble and thereby banning all future demonstrations because of the violence. The students promised an orderly demonstration so it should be interesting. Another

---

14 Dr. Melville Herskovits was a professor of anthropology at Northwestern University, where he later founded the first major program in African studies in the U.S. He later offered me a job as an anthropologist.

15 Henry W. "Ed" Bagley was the chief of the Associate Press bureau in Rio de Janeiro. He filed stories from all over the Amazon during WWII.

16 Ernâni Amaral Peixoto, was married to Vargas's daughter and was appointed "interventor", or governor, of the state of Rio de Janeiro.

17 Filinto Müller was the Chief of Police in the Federal District of Rio de Janeiro from 1933-42 under the Vargas dictatorship. He was a Nazi sympathizer, visited Germany as a guest of Heinrich Himmler, and created the system of repression and torture called the "Estado Novo." He lost his position when Vargas decided to support the Allies in WWII.

Brazilian ship was reported sunk but as yet unannounced by the Brazilian press.

The Trip to Espirito Santo

While the demonstrations and arrests were going on, Robert Holland and I decided that it would be fun to travel to the state of Espirito Santo, north of Rio.

We were up so early in the morning that the regular *bondes* weren't running, so we took the second class streetcars. They were a poor man's freight train and took everything and anyone who couldn't find transportation at that hour. One of the great things about Rio de Janeiro's open air surface transportation was the wonderful equality of it all. Most of the time the cars were too crowded to get in and get seated properly so you hung on the outside and watched that you didn't get washed off by some passing truck. In addition to collecting the fares, the conductor had to watch for traffic and yell, "*Olha direito,*" a sort of a "watch out" cry, to pedestrians.

The following diary notes record this trip:

July 3, 1942, continued

I am in a train headed for Vitória, capital of the state of Espirito Santo. It is 10:30 at night and we will have to sit up all night. When we got to the station, we found out that there were no reserved seats. Funny group or class of people who travel on these trains. They make a stab at asking people for ID but for everyone the guard asks he lets five go through.

July 4, 1942

Geologically, the Murundu zone is very interesting as it seems to be a transition zone of the northern part of the state of Rio de Janeiro. The Serra do Mar breaks it up and seems to have undulations of natural rock formations. The earth changes from sandy to the red earth of São Paulo. After Murucumdu the hills are much sharper. .... Sugar cane is in great abundance and we saw it being harvested; the population is predominantly Negro.

After a quiet ride through the sugar plantations of the state of Rio de Janeiro, we arrived across the river from Vitória, the capital of state of Espirito Santo. The train ended on the other side of the bay and we had to take a ferryboat across to the town. Vitoria is very beautiful with hills and valleys up to the bay. It is sort of a miniature Rio de Janeiro.

We took the American Vice Consul's address just in case we should accidentally on purpose pass his house. After a little innocent searching, imagine our surprise when we found it and a Fourth of July party. A small impressive house with chickens in the backyard and we announced ourselves. The Consul came out and greeted us with "Well, boys what sort of trouble are you in?" His name was Mr. [Percy G.] Kemp and he has been out of the States a long time. He called everybody Charley and Joe.

There were 13 Americans in town and all of them at the house of the consulate on the beach. What an assortment, like the Whitman sampler: there were three American naval attaches (spies), the Du Pont munitions salesmen, and a missionary. And a few others I could not account for. We had supper there and then went to some missionaries' house and had a nice conversation on the "Negro problem."

July 7, 1942

We took the bus to Colatina, where I am right now. The bus was loaded with people all colors of the rainbow, including blondes, Negroes, Spaniards, Indians, and mulattoes. We went through the Valley of Canaan, which has been immortalized in a novel by the Brazilian author [José Pereira da] Graça Aranha. The two cultured Englishmen in this novel discuss the turbulence of Brazilian life.

We went past German colonies and homes, with neat gardens, that seemed to be lifted right out of Bavaria. Cachoeira de Santa Leopoldina, Santa Teresa, where we stopped for coffee was really odd. The people all had ruddy complexions. The older women were buxom but in the German way not in the Brazilian way. Churches were all built in the German style.

Boy the roads are something terrific considering we wound up at about 8 o clock at night in Colatina. The center of town could hardly be seen it was so dimly lighted. It was like going into a town lit by 25 watt bulbs. We were led to a hotel but it looked so peculiar that we asked to be taken to the mayor's house. We had a letter of introduction to him.

The kid that was carrying our suitcase must have thought we were crazy. Outside the mayor's house we parked and opened the suitcase and took out the letter of introduction as well as a tie and then rang the bell. The perplexed young man tore off, convinced we were mad. It is kind of funny when you think of it.

The mayor was nonplussed, read our letter carefully, and showed us to the same hotel which was booked solid and so we had to look for another. The mayor said eat and then I'll see you later. He never showed up so we walked around town and went to sleep.

July 8, 1942

Last night the mayor was in a board meeting and could not break away. He turned out to be the captain of our boat and he welcomed us aboard this morning on a Mississippi type boat with a paddle wheel at the back. We boarded and headed down river for the town of Linhares.

The captain had the improbable name of Captain Trompowski. He gave us a letter to a fazendeiro [farmer] near Linhares whom we could stay with overnight. Obviously Trompowski is not Brazilian name. He surprised me by suddenly speaking English. Then he spilled out this fantastic tale.

He was a Russian Jew who had been working as an able bodied seaman when he had jumped ship in New York City. He attended Columbia University, majoring in Spanish, and then came the crash. He started boxing for money in the Golden Gloves. He later found work in Milwaukee, Wisconsin and was now piloting this river boat in Brazil. Wish I had found out more about him. He gave us a beautifully cut stone which really startled us.

The boat trip has been fascinating with delicious meals on the dock. We visited a pinga (sugar cane liquor) factory. This part of the country is headed for development. There were lots of little naked brats running around the decks but you get used to it.

What impressed the hell out of me was that the logs along the riverbank that would get up and walk away when the boat approached. That was my first introduction to real alligators (jacaré in Portuguese) in the river. Every once in a while the boat hit a sand bar that had shifted and half the crew would jump into the water with long poles as I watched nervously and ease the boat back into the main channel and on to its course.

We passed cocoa plantations and farms that reached down to the river's edge. I imagined that the plantations in the old south before the Civil War were like that. Whenever someone puts up a flag the captain heads for the landing but he said that he comes to shore only for 15 miles; the rest of the time they have to hail the boat and we would wait in the middle of the river. Yipes - we loaded a live pig in one mid-river stop. It gets damn cool on this river.

July 9, 1942

We ran aground in the middle of the Rio Doce. At first we were making such good progress that I thought we might get into Linhares that night. But as luck would have it after finishing what seemed like a $200 meal on the deck with a sunset thrown in for dessert the boat obligingly ran aground 5 or 6 miles outside of Linhares. That suited us fine as we got a nice cabin. We used the time to inspect the night skies and found the Southern Cross.

Note-taking on the Rio Doce, fall 1942.

I got up during the night as I could not sleep and saw a beautiful scene with silver crescent moon in a star lit sky reflected in the water. The sun rises are not spectacular here because there is so little dust in the air. It is now 7 a.m. in the morning and the men are still in the water - they don't seem to have gotten very far in getting the boat off the sand bar. That is fine as far as I am concerned. I hope they stay all afternoon.

They did not. In the usual mad and merry way, the boat got off the sand bar and arrived at [Campos dos] Goytacazes. There, we presented our letter to Djalma Paiva Gama, who is chief of the Experimental Station. He works with Cacao and I learned about the differences between Para and Creole Cacao: "spacing should be about 25 spaces apart." We stayed and had lunch with the young fellow at the ranch. They served us *capivara* (a rodent the size of a dog); it was an odd and funny tasting meat. They had a splendid lab but nobody to use it.

We were supposed to go Vitória on the 12 noon bus but it never appeared. Then the *fazenda* (farm) Chief grabbed us and offered us a ride - but before we could leave he suggested a crocodile hunt. Imagine me with a sun helmet, rifle over my arm, and real alligators. It would have been damn silly if we hadn't actually bumped into about 5 alligators. One of them was damn near 8 or 9 feet long. We were on the Rio Pequeno and headed for the Lagoa Juparanã. This was a spooky ride as the dense jungle was on both sides of the river and Robert and I in this Indian canoe. There were crocodiles jumping into river. We got back alive. Djalma Gama gave me some photos and a parrot which I hope to mount in São Paulo.

We left in the mayor's open Ford car and started a wild ride from Linhares to Santa Cruz. As the mayor happens to be a doctor we made some house calls along the way. We picked up some amazing things before we arrived in Santa Cruz. First some beans; then some bananas; then molasses; and then some cheese. We settled a legal dispute and finally gave some guy a prescription. I am now in some pensão in Santa Cruz.

July 10, 1942

Though we went to the best hotel in Vitória, Robert insisted on carrying his bags because the local kids would not a carry a bag for under a mil réis. Robert and I had had to fight them off when we arrived in Vitória from Santa Cruz; they just swarmed around us. Robert courageously put the suitcase on his shoulder to the dismay of all the waiting kids. Then at the moment of supreme triumph he lost his grip and the bag tumbled to earth amid the cheers and jeers of the brats. Boy was Robert's face red.

July 11, 1942

It is late in the afternoon and I have a beautiful splitting headache and a backache from the bus trip from Vitória where we left at 6 a.m. After a terrific row in the bus over our seats we settled down to what was the worst bus and the worst road of the entire trip. One has to be in good condition for this trip. We were we surprised by the size of this town. We had been expecting the worse and we found the hotel with toilet paper – rolls of it.

The police were out when we left Vitória. The Inspector just looked in the train window and just scowled at the passengers. We got up at 3:30 a.m. to catch the Rio train, which should arrive at 6:30 in the evening so that we will be able to get the night train to São Paulo, which leaves at 8:30.

So with another piece of Brazil under my belt, we returned to São Paulo. My view of Brazil was getting bigger, and I continued my studies at the university with a growing awareness that this country was a lot more complex than I had originally thought.

Back to School and Angst over the War

My stay in Brazil worried me. There was a war on, and I felt I should be fighting for my country. My diary notes reflect this:

July 13, 1942

I received a letter from my high school chum Dave. Due to my sister Annette's bubbling enthusiasm for any idea that strikes her fancy she told Dave that I was staying down here until the war is over. She told this to Dave who has been in the army for over a year now. As a result a good deal of bad blood. I have never been so damn angry in my life. The guys think I am shirking the war while I know damn well I am going back in four months but I feel naturally guilty that I am doing something wrong by staying down here to complete my school year. But that I will do job or no job. I am going back to the U.S.A. after November. I'll try and explain more when I calm down but I do feel like slugging someone.

July 17, 1942

The long awaited pop off in the government made headlines in the late afternoon papers. The changes in the government though important seem not to be the focal point in the excitement that seems to have been raised. The fact is that three alleged fascists - Müller, the Chief of Police; The Minister of Justice; and [Lourival] Fontes head of DIP - were all removed; it seems on the surface to be a victory for democracy but what gripes the hell out of everyone was the manner in which it was done. And the manner in which the Brazilians are receiving the news. I saw little excitement today in the streets. When the first news flashes came out the people didn't seem to give a damn.

Someone remarked to me that it was more intelligent to discuss this situation at home and vent your feelings there. It is a lot safer too. The events look good on the surface but it also reveals a terrible weakness in the government when they ought to be strong. The most surprising to me was the DIP change. There had been rumors about the others and a lot of gossip but nothing regarding Lourival Fontes. One keeps ones fingers crossed as you see the number of military men who are an unknown quantity. It is funny how as early as July 2nd we knew in Rio all about changes.

July 18, 1942

I seem to have made an error in my calculations about the changes in government. The Chief of Police seems to have been mixed up in the revolution or demonstrations of last October which were very liberal and in some manner spoke of land distribution for the poor. Some say he is a Luís Carlos Prestes[18] supporter. Students didn't react at all, not in the class I attended in the afternoon.

---

[18] Luís Carlos Prestes was the leader of the Communist opposition to the Vargas dictatorship. Vargas imprisoned him in 1935 and deported his German, Jewish wife to Nazi Germany, where she died in a concentration camp. Vargas released Prestes from prison in 1945, but he was persecuted again by later regimes.

Gave an English lesson and then went to a party at Dr. Lorch's. I thought I would have a lousy time but it turned out to be damn good. There were some of the richest girls in Brazil present. Why in the hell can't they be pretty and have some personality. They seem as emotional and interesting as a dead herring.

I drank too much last night and amazingly did not get high. Colder than hell again last night; oh boy it really gets cold!

July 22, 1942

One of these days I am going to learn a lesson but strongly. It is often said that knowing something is half the battle. But I'm afraid that some people such as me take it as if it were the whole battle. Unless I learn the respective place of amusement in regard to work, I am going to be in one hell of a mess. But the fact that a girl said let's go to the movies and I did not have the backbone to say no that I did not want to go to the movies. And add insult her mother was there and went with us.

Went to Moore McCormack to see about a passage back home. It looks like it will be difficult. But I am resolved. Killing a few Jap's and Nazis is as pleasant a way to leave this world as any. A hell of a lot pleasanter than living with them as bosses.

July 23, 1942

Went to my morning classes and I find the course on the Negro in Brazil the most interesting. Received a 5th Columnist poster. They seem to have some effect on the German across the street. He displays Nazi banners on German victory days. The one hour history lesson was full of stuff about Portugal so it did not stick. Went to a dentist; he is damn expensive at 40 mil réis an hour.

July 26, 1942

Just thrown back on my own thoughts about home and then everything here takes on a nice mysterious glow. It should and it does. I am over 5000 miles from home and in the midst of world upheaval that is smoldering all around me and I have as yet have not burned my fingers.

I am trying like the devil to get home. Yet you find yourself torn between two currents. And here I never let myself do that nor do I think I should that I am living on borrowed time.

School has been pretty much the same but I have been having a hell of time coping with the food. The weather continues to be cold and I sleep with a sweater on and warm stockings. I dream of a warm house.

I finally contacted my old students and one paid me 100 mil réis which I promptly gave to Robert to pay for my vacation. The other part I gave to the dentist.

Saturday went to a goodbye party given for Barbara Hadley and I hope to see her in the States. She teaches at Smith College[19].

I tried to get a date for Sunday but was very unsuccessful. Edite is off the list but definitely. I generally still think that the Brazilians are a damn hospitable bunch of people. G'nite. Sometimes I have that funny feeling as if I have got to finish what I am doing and get home and go to sleep even though I am at home.

July 30, 1942

Last night I went to dinner at Margaret Churst's house. A rich dizzy little girl. The atmosphere was one that I have read about in books but I have never seen. Rather rich people discussing others in terms of initials of R.B. or J.M. I almost burst out laughing at the conversations at the dinner table. They spoke of what they would do if they had 12,000 contos [worth approximately $50]. I had to laugh again when the rich girls said money doesn't mean anything. I doubt that I would want anything that I haven't got now.

We discussed books and the latest dissa and datta. Then we played poker for a few chips and drank brandy just like in the movies. I felt it was at first unadulterated phooey. Then the lights went off and I got home in the deep fog around midnight. I slept under a heavy quilt and got up a 7:30.

Breakfast was two cups of coffee and two rolls and butter. Took the street car at 8 and gave Dr. Sarfaim a lesson from 8:30 to 9:30. We are reading *Elmer Gantry*[20]. Boy I am nuts to have him read this but he pays 200 mil réis a month.

Went to class at 10 o'clock and the professor did not show up. Walked over to the União Cultural and returned a book and then returned for my 11 o'clock class in Portuguese language. At 12, I went home for lunch – noodles, salad, meat, rice, and mamão. Lay down for a nap and got up at 1:30 and then my 2:00 o'clock class – and no professor there either. Dirceu and I went window shopping until 3:30. I then went to the library at the Escola Livre and studied until 4:45 and then went to the Lewis class in mathematical logic. Took street car home and met that cute girl that I think is damn appealing. Waiting for supper now.

---

19 She turned out to be Mrs. Stanley Stein, a friend and neighbor in Princeton.

20 *Elmer Gantry* is a satirical novel by Sinclair Lewis, written in 1926.

August 4, 1942

Wow August is here. Won't be long before summer time is nearly over – got myself reversed winter is nearly over and spring around the corner. Brazilian public opinion still considers itself as neutral in the war. As a result of Waldo Frank's attacks a lot of Brazilians began to talk and said what the hell if the allies win ok, Brazil gains. If the Axis wins the government falls and so one comes out in favor of the Axis and it's all over. Phooey!!

The Trip to Goiás

In August, there was a break between classes and Paul Oechsli and I decided we would make a trip by ourselves to the interior of Brazil. The use of the word "interior" demands some explaining - if you went out of the large cities you were sort of entering Indian country, or at least areas that were not well known even to most Brazilians. In other words, it was an adventure. We decided to go north through the state of Minas Gerais to the state of Goiás.

We took the Mogiana narrow-gage railroad (Companhia Mogiana de Estradas de Ferro) to the change of trains, which took us to the town of Riberão Preto, still in the state of São Paulo. (In Portuguese the place you change trains is called a *baldeação*, which sounds much more impressive in Portuguese than it does in English.) We all got off the train and had lunch. They said they would call us when the train was ready. Lunch was set up in a long table in the station and we fell to it. The men wore linen traveling coats to protect their clothing from the ashes of the engine, which made for an odd sight.

Lunch over, the trip continued. The pace was slower and there was one occasion when the train could not get up a hill because of the steep grade. The engineer tried twice, then ordered the second class passengers off the train while we tried again to make the ascent. We finally made it and we watched as the second class passengers climbed back in.

These are the sort of stories that we heard about the train service. Once a train pulled into a small town and the mayor, a brass band, and young girls with flowers came out to greet the train. What was all the excitement about? Well, this was the first time in 15 years that the train had arrived on time. All well and good but the engineer had to admit that this was yesterday's train. Probably apocryphal.

Traveling by *jardineira* in Goiás.

Once on the Mogiana line things proceeded at slower tempo. The train was on a narrow gauge railroad track that seemed like a Toonerville Trolley[21]. It huffed and puffed its way into a station, but a citizen failed to get off the tracks in time and was struck. The train came to grinding halt. The authorities came out and attempted to arrest the engineer and it was touch and go if we would be able to continue with our trip.

The next stop was at Uberlândia and from there we took a *jardineira*, which is a sort of small bus, to Rio Verde in the southern part of the state of Goiás. I remembered vividly that as the bus tore down the road the driver sighted a wild animal, to my memory it was a capibara[22]. The hunt was on. The bus ran off the road and we caroomed around as we chased the animal. The fellow next to me said "*Com permiso*" (with your permission), pulled out a .38 caliber pistol, leaned across me, and started shooting at the capibara. He didn't hit it and we got back on the road and continued to Rio Verde. We were welcomed by Dr. Duarte Caeser.

I had bought a small suitcase that was made out of goat skin. The goat it was taken from must have been in heat because

---

21 The Toonerville Trolley refers to a comic strip from 1908 to 1955, with a small trolley that met all the commuter trains.

22 A capibara (*capivara* in Portuguese) is the world's largest rodent, the size of the small dog.

everywhere we went the goats would try to try mount the damn thing and copulate with it.

After exploring Rio Verde for a few days, we traveled to Bom Jesus de Goiás on top of a truck loaded with gasoline tins and sacks of rice. We passed Caraíba, Rio Bonito, Ponte Funda, and Vianópolis[23]. At Bom Jesus the only accommodations were in a mud hut. We then back-tracked to Uberlândia to get the train to Araguari. When we got there, the guards detained us, thinking we were Germans. We had to have a long talk to convince them we were Norte Americanos. Luckily for us, the train ran late and we left our encounter with the police with time to spare.

The conductor gave us second class seats because he could not change the bills we had. Then we had to prove that we had a right to travel although we didn't have any *salvo conduto* or safe conduct pass. War hadn't been declared yet, and many Brazilians were not sure what side they were on. A sense of tension was thick in the air.

We got into Anápolis, the capital of the state of Goiás, at ten o'clock at night and were promptly treated to tea by the Faunstone family, who worked in the city as medical missionaries. Paul's parents had been missionaries in Indonesia - and that made us welcome. Nothing ever tasted so good as the tea they served that night.

Dr. Faunstone had a hospital and training school for nurses. Paul and I had to sleep in a small room next to the dormitory that held thirty nurses, who bolted the door due to some unsubstantiated fears for their virginity. We ran into Joan Lowell, an American actress who was famous for her faux-autobiography *Cradle of The Deep*. We also met a Mrs. Bowen there who told us wild stories about superstition within the area.

(Fast forward to a reception at the home of former ambassador Flávio Miragaia Perri, the Brazilian Consul in New York, on East 78th Street just off Central Park. The date was February 2002 and I mentioned the fact that I knew the hospital in Anápolis. Luiz Tupy Caldas de Moura, Brazil's Deputy Permanent Representative at the United Nations, admitted he was born in that hospital.)

---

23 I found a reference to this last in an article by Floyd Greenleaf, "A Different Kind of Bandeirante." Dr. Greenleaf was a professor at Southern Adventist University, where he wrote two volumes on the history of the Seventh Day Adventists in Latin America and the Caribbean.

Brazil declared war on the Axis powers while we were in Anápolis. We wondered what this would mean but nothing new happened. Someone had given us an introduction to Dr. Herbert Levy[24]; one of his men in the region offered us a truck ride that was going north so that we could see the future site of Brasília. People offered us land for sale but the 50 cents in our pocket was not enough to buy.

We started home to São Paulo because classes were starting again. We were weary but confident that we had looked into the future of western Brazil.

---

24 Dr. Herbert Levy was the owner and chairman of *Gazeta Mercantil*, Brazil's most important business daily. He was oneof the backers of President Jánio Quadros' political campaign.

Chapter 5. Fall Classes and a Real Job

In September I resumed classes at both universities. At USP, I continued to study the geography of Brazil with Prof. Aroldo de Azevedo and the history of Brazil with Prof. Alfredo Ellis, Jr. At the Escola Livre, I studied Brazilian Ethnology with Prof. Herbert Baldus, the Development of the Brazilian Negro with Prof. Donald Pierson, the Study of Society, Principles of Social Anthropology, and the Portuguese language. While I tried desperately to keep a diary, I obviously didn't try hard enough, as my notes for my last semester as a student in Brazil are rather skimpy.

September 26, 1942

Sort of flopped again on writing but sometimes you get going and everything happens so fast that you can't grab on to anything solid to slow you down. Everything seems fluid like a bad Salvador Dali painting.

I was 22 years old yesterday. Still don't give a tinker's dam for ceremony but I have to admit that the party thrown for me last night was honestly one of the happiest of my life.

Sitting in the pretty garden in the house on Alameda Tiete in the sun now. I really feel funny. Gosh can you imagine the school term got a cake baked in the form of the school and then had two figures: one of Donald Duck and the other of Joe Carioca[25]. Damn if they ask me to

[25] José Carioca is a cartoon parrot who appears in the 1942 Disney film *Saludos Amigos* alongside Donald Duck, in a short segment entitled *Aquarela do Brasil* ("Watercolor of Brazil"). *Saludos* was a product of the FDR administration's Good Neighbor Policy, which aimed to increase both diplomatic and cultural goodwill between the U.S.A. and South American nations. *It's All True*, a failed Orson Welles project discussed in Chapter 8, was also produced under the auspices of this policy.

make a speech but all I could say was "let's eat the cake." Of all the times when I should have said something – I didn't.

Dona Noemi Silveira Rudolpher (the psychiatrist) was there. Much to my surprise she is considered one of the First Ladies of Brazil. Mrs. Culver [wife of John Culver, head of the IBEU] was there also. A hell of a lot of assistants to the professors were also present.

It does not feel I am 5,000 miles away from home. It's strange to have everyone conversing in two languages. Well I am still in the honeymoon of my years of the 20s and using the years as they should be used. We danced the Samba that everyone calls the hottest thing. Wow you really must have self control for that. (Note to myself in 2005: I know the samba can be sensuous dance but at a birthday party? You must have been joking.)

I have been keeping up with my school work. I am thinking about going home but don't have anything definite yet.

Have I introduced the family here? Mr. Edwardo Carlos Magalhães, Dona Leda who is what we would call the head of the house. There are four kids in the house and a dog who looks like of corn fluff and is called "peepoka" [pipoca, or popcorn]. Nice but it gives me a homesick feeling.

Sept. 30, 1942

I am sitting in my 2 o'clock class and Professor [Alfredo] Ellis is reeling off the names of all the governors of Brazil from the first one in 1613 - 1617 Gaspar de Souza and so on and on. The room is much like the class rooms in an American university. I wish I could take a girl out for a coke at 3 o'clock but one there are no cokes here and two the girls are unavailable and three you are crazy. OK.

Tried out for a play yesterday. I think I got the part. We are going to have a black out Friday night. As this is the first one, it should be entertaining.

Remember Edith about whom I wrote about two books ago - the one that biked over to my place? She came over again and we went to the movies. Yipes she smooches and I will keep my fingers crossed.

October 4, 1942

Listening to the radio and the Jockey Club program which plays nice music. The room is fixed up rather nicely as an office. Am doing my weekly clean up. Yesterday I gave a geography talk with movies about Goiás. Not very good but it served a purpose I hope. I hope I get a grade out of the course.

Had a class until 4:30 then left with Mieva Akoree Abola from Minas Gerais. Had two cafezinhos [espressos] and took the Jardim Europe bonde going home. I had supper and then went to Edith's house and studied until 10:00 o'clock. She is a nice kid but a Brazilian woman in all her habits. Friday night was blackout night and I met her for a while. This morning she surprised me by popping over on her bicycle and we went out to study somewhere.

I have been preparing the Goiás trip for classroom presentation and also the report on the Negro. This has developed into a problem because I have been offered a research project if I stay in Brazil three more months than I planned. Dr. John Culver director of the Institute [Instituto Brasil–Estados Unidos] says "go home." I don't know what to do. I have to settle this in my own way. Boy but it sure is a nice battle royal. I saw an opera by Carlos Gomes Guarani Thursday night.

Brazil and the Early Years of World War II

In general, Brazil and its people favored the Allies. From the time I read of the attack on Pearl Harbor until I left to join the army in 1944, I never felt any hostility toward Americans on the part of the Brazilians. Throughout my school year there was only sympathy for our cause. However, my attempts to get the United States government to send me back home always ended in failure, as the people at the Consulate told me that there were more pressing concerns than the repatriation of Jordan Young to join the army.

I watched the war with frustration. In 1942 we were losing the war, yet the U.S.A. made sure that Brazil would remain a loyal ally. Getúlio Vargas, the Brazilian dictator, was in favor of the democratic forces fighting Hitler; his generals, seeing the successes of the German fighting machine, were pro-Axis. Brazil had already granted the U.S.A. air and naval bases in the country: Belém on the Amazon and Fortaleza, Recife, and Natal in the northeast were all staked out as U.S. bases. This had not been an easy sell for the Brazilian people, as Brazil had been economically and politically manhandled by the British in the 19th century. They were wary of another foreign power trying to make a foothold.

Economic aid programs were also being pushed by the United States. Nelson Rockefeller[26] organized the Institute of Inter-

26 Nelson Rockefeller was later the Governor of New York and the Vice President of the U.S. under Gerald Ford.

American Affairs (IIAA), which he ran as coordinator. The Brazilians viewed this work with some suspicion as Americans began to show up and flood the country as nutrition specialists, sanitary engineers, port workers, and malaria technicians. Many Brazilians felt they could do this work themselves, and wondered if the Americans would leave after the war.

I Get a Job

With war raging in Europe, my academic year in São Paulo came to a close in November 1942. It was time to do something and I began to look for some war-related work. I became aware that the Institute of Inter-American Affairs (IIAA) was looking for Americans when my roommate Paul resigned from the Consulate and got a job with its Food and Nutrition Division. He suggested I apply to the Health and Sanitation Division, which just might need someone who had been trained in sociology, so off I went to Rio de Janeiro.

This division was part of the push by the American and Brazilian governments to improve health and sanitation conditions in Brazil's rural areas. (Paul's particular operation was related to improving agricultural techniques.) Of course – in both cases - they focused on areas that would help the American war effort, areas such as rubber in the Amazon and iron ore in the south. Though the Brazilians were initially suspicious of the range of the projects, such misgivings were apparently smoothed over when it became clear that U.S. interests in the war had limited Latin American objectives.

The IIAA was a Rockefeller operation and as such was at odds with the State Department, which did not like the enthusiasm and the unstructured Rockefeller-style way in which things were done. Though most of its employees, such as the American sanitary engineers and agricultural technicians, were recruited in the U.S.A., it appeared that local help could be hired in Brazil without getting Washington's approval. To this day I don't know what got into the head of Arthur Way, the man who employed me, to take a chance on this American.

During my interview I asked Arthur if there was opportunity to work outside of the cities, in the rural interior. This must have been an odd request for him and perhaps that is why he hired me. At first he couldn't figure out a title for me, but as I was registered as student of sociology at the Escola Livre he settled on "Rural Sociologist" and I was officially hired.

Thus begin the adventures of Jordan Young, Rural Sociologist, with the Health and Sanitation Division of the Coordinator of Inter American Affairs. Of course the real Jordan Young was still a junior student at the University of Illinois majoring in Latin American history - at least, that's what I felt like.

Undated journal entry, late 1942

In Rio the last few days I did not have time to write as I was busy wasting my money. I took Pat out and it is fun dating an English girl. Took Louise out and it was not fun dating an American high school girl just because they were of the female sex. It is startling in Rio to see the American soldiers: army, navy, and air force walking around in uniform. There is heaps of material for short stories in Rio if some just takes the time out to write them.

Saturday night going down to the Urca[27] nightclub and sat and watched the show with about 70 couples trying look happy and enchanted, on a postage cigarette stamp sized dance floor. The lights going on all along Copacabana Beach are always fascinating. The gin and tonic parties, Jane Braga, and all the people whom "have you heard the latest" make little chills run up and down my spine. The beach club for Americans on Copacabana Beach - a clip joint "but all the Americans go – so my dear you simply must." B.S. Eating at the Copacabana Palace and feeling like you are in a morgue with about half the bodies are alive and the other half are zombies without rum. Seeing people eat the gravy and stew. Lunch at the airport and the super sophisticated 16 ½ year old star dates or American secretary caught in the war and scattered to the far corners of the globe to keep up with the American executives.

Sunset at Arpoador[28], the spray on the rocks. Meeting Americans at the Luxor, the lack of decent American girls to date. The milkshakes and ice cream cones at the 5 &10 cent store. Air conditioned offices giving you colds every week. And then the American bombers flying over Rio every day, silly modern buildings looking like a page out of the Grand Concourse of the Bronx, and the visiting characters who lived in those and now living down here in a funny upside down world.

---

27 Urca is a wealthy neighborhood of Rio at the base of Sugarloaf Mountain by the yacht club.

28 Arpoador is the spit of land that separates Copacabana and Ipanema beaches in Rio.

First Assignment

My first IIAA assignment was in the mining area of Brazil. I journeyed to the town of Itabira do Mato Dentro (literally "Itabira Inside the Forest"), which was located east of Cauê in the state of Minas Gerais. There, the U.S.A. was helping Brazil mine Cauê, a mountain of high-grade iron ore. The company that owned the operation, Companhia Vale do Rio Doce, was a semi-governmental organization. They were also upgrading the railroad track that went from the iron mountain in Minas Gerais to Vitória, seaport capital of the state of Espirito Santo.

A typical colonial mining town in Brazil hit its high point around 1710, when gold and silver from Latin America could be found around the world. Ever since then these towns have been marking time, waiting for history to catch up. Mule trains moved through Itabira with leather saddle-bags carrying supplies for miners. The sparks from the mules' hooves as they clashed on the iron ore in the cobblestone streets gave off an eerie glint on gray days. The town was a hilly up-and-down affair, with old colonial buildings perched over the road. The women and girls draped themselves over the iron balconies, which loomed over the street,

With a pair of officials from Companhia Valle do Rio Doce (CVRD), the company in charge of mining operations in Itabira.

to watch the world go by. Church processions would wind their way through the streets with a Saint carried by the men of Itabira.

The empty, dusty nature of the town on hot afternoons reminded me of a Wild West movie. Carlos Drummond de Andrade, a nationally-known Brazilian poet, was born in Itabira. In 1928 he wrote a wonderfully evocative poem about the town called "Confidência do Itabirano":

Alguns anos vivi em Itabira
Princpalmente nasci em Itabira
Por isso sou triste, orgulhoso de ferro
Noventa por cento de ferro nas calçadas
Oitenta por cento de ferro nas almas.
E esse alheamento do que na vida é porosidade e comunicaçâo

This is my rough translation:

For some years I lived in Itabira
Foremost I was born in Itabira
That's why I'm sad and proud of iron
Ninety percent iron in the streets
Eighty percent iron in the souls
And was ignored in life and it is in my pores and communication

The local mayor and I had long conversations on the state of the world. The local padre would tell me stories about the people in town, and even in my young and self-assured state I somehow felt he knew more about the world than I did. The dusty horses and mules of course were tethered in front of the stores. You would hear shouts of "*mula mula*" to get the trains started again.

Mr. St. Clair.

I was a serous young man and went around asking all sorts of questions. The mayor of the town took time off to pose in front of his drugstore. Mr. Homer St. Clair was a

Hercules Powder Company representative in town and knew everybody and everything that was going on. I've often wondered about the role of our international munitions salesmen between World War I and World War II. Did they report to the Embassy? It would certainly make sense as their German counterparts did the same.

My job was to teach the locals about victory gardens and how to use sanitary facilities. I was to study the conditions of the rural workers and write a report on what was going on in the area. I leased a mule and rode it to work every morning.

The people were the rural poor of Brazil. Many came from rural areas of Minas Gerais and others from the state of Bahia. I tried to teach them sanitary methods; most wanted to use the great outdoors to relieve themselves saw toilets as an unnecessary complication. Some of them used the toilets seats we gave them as frames for family portraits. My mule and I used to show up daily to see if they had complied with our request. I did not get very far. I inspected where people lived and reported to headquarters in Rio de Janeiro on their bad toilet training.

After reading my reports on my findings over a month's period, the IIAA, in its infinite wisdom, decided that I was ready for bigger and better things. Maybe a change of climate would be good for me, so they sent me further north.

Migrant mine workers in Itabira.

Chapter 6. Fortaleza and the Northeast (Spring 1943)

My next assignment by the Institute of Inter-American Affairs (IIAA) was the vast northeast of Brazil. My diary entries record my arrival and settling in.

March 4, 1943[29]

Yesterday I flew 1800 miles from Rio de Janeiro straight through the interior of country to the state of Ceará. We went about 200 miles an hour at about 12,000 feet up. Things don't look so interesting from that height. We had a nice box lunch but too much heavy greasy food. I could now just about picture what was going on in that hermetically sealed plane, people eating their box lunches, half of them asleep with their mouths open just like in a continental Greyhound bus. After this trip I will never again feel romantic at the sight of a huge airplane way up in the stratosphere.

The airline was a Brazilian one (Panair do Brasil) using an American Lockheed Lodestar plane. They take off at an amazing speed. Over the first part of Minas Gerais you get the feeling that the state was splattered like a tomato against a wall. Little lumps and dumps rising all over. The first thing that attracted me about Fortaleza was the nice flatness of the town after living these last years in hilly country; I actually welcomed the flat stuff.

---

[29] I have been finding diaries like mad. This one was found on November 23, 2001 and it I was written in March 1943. A little under 50 years ago – a half century has passed. I feel, as I read them, that I am reading a wonderful strange diary of person that I know and yet I don't know. It is a fascinating to see yourself as you were 50 year ago. It is an odd and rare privilege. - Jordan M. Young, 2011

When we landed in Fortaleza [the capital of Ceará], the military field was in evidence with sleek shiny deadly bombers scattered around. They seemed to have learned nothing from the fact that in war time it is bad practice to leave planes lying around in compact groups.

As a tired traveler I checked into Palace Hotel located on a quaint square lined with old trees. I had a cold so went to bed at 7:30 last night – golly if you let your mind wander you can feel very lost. It is only when I get to look at a map do I get a little worried about the magnitude of the changes I am experiencing.

Fortaleza was a sleepy coastal city tacked on to a huge area that resembled the desert of southwest Arizona. It was not really a port, as incoming cargo had to be unloaded from a lighter and then ferried to land. It had the feeling of a frontier town despite the fact that it had been settled for hundreds of years. The beach that stretched for miles south of the town was known as the Praia de Iracema. The streets were lined with the type of trees you associate with the tropical south seas - beautiful tall arching palms that bent over the beach. For this North American the sight of those palm trees seemed like a South Sea novel come to life.

The beach was made famous by José de Alencar's 1865 novel *Iracema*, which tells the tale of a lovely Indian woman called Iracema who fell in love with a Portuguese soldier. The story resembles James Fennimore Cooper's tales of the North American frontier. Alencar describes Iracema as having lips of honey and I learned the first few lines of the novel, which went:

Alem muito alem daquela serra ainda azula no horizonte nacie Iracema. A virgin dos labio de mel, que tinha os cabelos mais negros que a asa da graûna e mais longos que o seu talhe de palmeira.

And my rough English translation:

Further, much further than the mountain that shimmers on the horizon, Iracema was born, the virgin with honeyed lips and black hair.

The words burned themselves into my memory so much so that, now, some sixty years later, I can still repeat the lines from that story. The beach had been named after this memorable character.

Life was good in Fortaleza. Strolling at night along the Praia de Iracema, the local kids would climb up the tall coconut trees and bring down coconuts. They would lop off the top and lace the coconut milk with a Brazilian brandy called *cachaça*, and we would proceed home with a pleasant buzz.

The northeast of Brazil defied description; its persistent droughts created a scene like the 1930's Dust Bowl magnified 100 times. We would gather workers who were undernourished and suffering from malnutrition and get them properly fed before making them into a ragtag army of rubber workers to be sent up the Amazon. I arrived and the staff was surprised to see me; they had not asked for me, I was just sent. We had a hospital there at the edge of town and my boss was the famous anthropologist Charles Wagley[30].

Working for SESP

The SESP (Serviço Especial de Saúde Pública) was the Portuguese name for our organization, which translates as the Special Public Health Service. The branch in Fortaleza was responsible for getting masses of men up to the rubber plantations of the Amazon. They were called the Rubber Army and came in from the drought-stricken interior in rags seeking food and shelter. Our job was to provide both.

We sent about 25,000 men to the Amazon; of these, 17,000 to 20,000 never returned. Some of them disappeared, and others drifted back through the arid back-country to get home again to Ceará. Some 7,000 were never accounted for.[31]

Later on when I was working in the Amazon project I saw where we had been sending those men. It wasn't a nice place; the incoming workers lived in malaria-infested squalor, as wage slaves to the local rubber barons, but perhaps anything was better than the slow death through starvation that awaited them if they had stayed put. At the time, Brazil seemed to have people to burn.

Here are two journal entries that give the flavor of my life in Fortaleza.

---

[30] Charles Wagley trained at Columbia University in anthropology under Franz Boas, and specialized in Central America and then Brazil. He convinced the U.S. government to send aid to Brazil to encourage rubber production for the war effort.

[31] As of 2006 the rubber soldiers in Brazil were still fighting for recognition and compensation for their work. The New York Times estimates that over 55,000 men were recruited from the Northeast of Brazil and sent to work harvesting and processing rubber in the Amazon region, as part of an effort created by an agreement between the U.S. and Brazilian governments. When the war ended, many men were not released to return home, but continued to work as wage slaves.

March 5, 1943

Good morning. Yesterday eating alone in the hotel got me down so I got a little bottle of wine and felt very good about it.

Went to various camps yesterday. My first visit was to SEMP, which was the camp for men going to the Amazon. The place is called the Hospedaria do Prado. There the single men are placed in long straw covered barracks and sleep in hammocks. The first impression I had was that the men were prisoners and were there against their will but they are not. They were there on their own free will. They looked, however, like the prisoners from Devil Island with big straw floppy hats. The camp looks very temporary. There are straw roofs on the all the barracks except the hospital which has tile. The kitchen looked spacious but was open for flies of which there were plenty. The SESP here takes care of health and sanitation and sees that the toilets are clean and food decently prepared.

I next went to the hospital, where for the first time in my life I saw children that were on the verge of death from starvation. They are people from the families being sent up by the serviço de imigração. This includes only families of which about 600 persons were sent off yesterday to [the state of] Amazonas. The doctors looked very competent here. Then I went to the Hospedaria [Hostel] dos immigrants, which was well set up.

Barracks where northeastern rubber workers were gathered before being sent into the Amazon.

Rubber workers at a camp.

March 6, 1943

I have felt the undercurrent of war here more than any other place I have been in a long time. I was startled when about 50 American aviators turned up at the hotel yesterday on their way to Africa with flying fortresses.

This is a very tropical town. Sometimes you begin to sweat just sitting in a chair. It is the kind of place that you string a hammock in the living room and fall asleep in it and then wake up about 3 a.m., take a drink of water, play the radio, and go back to bed. Most of rooms have mosquito nets but after the first night you get used to them. Almost any town in the world can become dull and prosaic if you let it become so. This town has a lot of charm and pleasantness but if one stays at the hotel and sits in the lobby there is nothing that can make you realize there is nothing very distinctive or different about this town then there is in Hoboken.

Went to the beach yesterday and saw a few young girls. I firmly resolved to move out to the beach if at all possible. It seems that I am stationed here permanently and therefore hope to take up housekeeping at the *praia* [beach]. I moved into Palace Hotel and am now sharing a room with a guy named Shoemaker from ADP (Airport Development

> Program), a private operation that built the airports for both the Brazilian and American governments[32].
>
> These are very dangerous times for me. There are no restraints on me and the climate is seductive and lets me do anything I want. Sort of gives you a strange feeling and to hell with rest of the world. If I can manage to get a house and a few nice looking servants then may be able to do that but not now. The civilized modern part of world is too close at times - yet fantastically far also. But I am really afraid of this place more than I am of any other – it sort of gets under your skin; very Tropical, too tropical for me.
>
> First impression that I had of the people was that they paid less attention to the girls then they do in Rio or São Paulo. People seem to be more intelligent but there is a lot of begging in the streets. Carnival starts tonight and I am not the least bit enthused about going to dances in formal clothes. I guess I'll go but am not too enthused about it.

In Fortaleza I saw many sights for the first time: a dead person with candles around the body in the hospital; an elderly man who had died of starvation; a woman with a tiny whisk broom sweeping up some grains of rice that had fallen from a sack that was being unloaded from a truck. Poverty and hunger were the norm there.

Charles Wagley was head of the project and he told me my job was to write the monthly reports. This kind of paperwork was the very thing that I had been running away from. Then there was Dr. Hyman Zuckerman, an American doctor from Brooklyn who was to be the medical liaison with the Brazilians. He had a ball down there. He later became personal physician to Brazilian President Jusceleno Kubitschek. Finally, there was some guy whose job was undefined, but from his demeanor and the sorts of questions he would ask around the office, we all assumed he was from the FBI.

Once I was sent on a trip to Sobral and Tianguá, in the interior of Ceará. A more desolate landscape I have never seen in my life; it was a moonscape, with only a tree here or there to color the desolation. I could see why people emigrated to the city; at least there you had people to talk to and share experiences, but out here was nothing. During a lunch break in Tianguá we sat on our haunches and watched a dog cross the street. It was the most

---

[32] The Airport Development Program was run by U.S.-owned Pan American Airways and started building airfields in Latin America in 1940. Its first airport in Brazil was built in Amapá, in the northernmost part of Brazil, as part of a series of airfields to connect the U.S. with Africa.

exciting event of the day, and we laid bets if the dog would make it. It was that kind of a town.

The pensão I lived in after my time with the Air Corps.

Now I had the first real money I ever had in my life (I think it was about seventy-five dollars a week), so I did odd things like getting a massage every afternoon. I thought this sort of frivolous personal expense was quite exotic. I also bought a horse. I don't remember if I ever rode on it but I thought it would be a good idea to clop around the beach on this nag. Then I bought a monkey, which lasted a week because it had the annoying habit of peeing while he was clamped on to my arm.

Sex never did seem to come up. I tried to score with the family girls but it was a strikeout every time. There was a young secretary named Marina, but she was from a good family and by this time I had learned the taboo of the good "family girls" so I did not try to make any progress with her. The prostitutes in the red light district were just too far gone for my taste.

Life with the U.S. Army Air Corps

I rented a room in a house right smack on the beach but I soon moved, as it was a spooky place with a swimming pool that had too many slimy things living in it. I lasted one month and then moved in with the U.S. Army Air Corps. There was a squadron that was stationed at the Fortaleza airport with about twenty P-40's. Their job was to search for German submarines that might threaten the shipping lanes of the south Atlantic. The number of German subs that they found on the coast of Brazil was pretty nearly nil, and none of them spoke any Portuguese. The pilots felt pretty isolated in Fortaleza, and asked me to move in with them. I thought that was a great idea, especially since they had all that wonderful American food and drink from the PX in Miami.

While these young Air Force pilots might not have discovered many German subs, they soon found the Red Light district in Fortaleza. On slow nights it seemed that the whole district had moved into our house on the beach. I don't know why but they put me off limits to the ladies of the night. The girls might fool around with me but whenever I got overheated they backed off. It was a rule the pilots enforced strictly, as I was considered too young or something.

There were many scenes that I don't believe even when reading my diary for the period. One night they had a wild orgy in the house when I was sleeping, and I woke up to find a nude woman who was screaming and could not let go of the refrigerator door, on account of an electrical current from the fridge. I managed to get the thing unplugged and she tumbled to the floor, yelling Portuguese curses at me. Another time I awoke to a young girl busy putting flowers in my hair.

Admiral Jonas H. Ingram, the South Atlantic Commander of the Southern Atlantic Force of the U.S. Fleet, scheduled a visit to the base. An elaborate dinner was planned at our house, but the pilots forgot to tell the "girls" not to come that night. About 10 p.m., as dinner was just getting started, we heard taxis pull up to the house and the women burst into the room. It had been a slow night and they decided to pay us a visit. There was a moment of embarrassing silence. The screams of "*Ola, querido*" [hello, darling!] were barely out the mouths of the damsels when the captain in charge of the Air Force squadron jumped to his feet, turned to me, and said in a tone that I will never forget, "Jordan, you speak Portuguese. Would you please tell your friends to leave." Heavy emphasis on "your friends." I told the women as much and they left quietly.

I moved shortly after that and entered into a dull but definitely quieter boarding house on the beach.

March 7, 1943

I realize that I am not good at making at contacts but I feel for some reason or other if I am in Fortaleza after 6 months, let's say through September '43, I am going to have to do something drastic. I don't know why I dislike this town. Perhaps it is because I am living in a hotel which is bad anywhere but here it is especially depressing. This is the carnival period and even though I went to a dance last night I didn't enjoy myself as I should have.

The war is seen here more strongly than any other place. Like the other night I heard about the boys who were just a few days out from the states and bound for Africa. One of them cracked up in the jungle and the natives would not accept any money. This was told to me in the praça [plaza] in front of the hotel where some Americans (guards from the air field) were drinking with the Brazilians.

I am sharing the shower in this place with Shoemaker. The Black Out is an on and off thing. I wore patent leather shoes for the dance and am feeling very sheepish about it. I can't quite put my finger on it but this is a super tropical atmosphere here; it's only 3 ½ degrees from the equator and is cooled by trade winds. You actually see Americans sick from staying here too long. I am going to try and move out to the beach as soon as I can. If possible rent a house.

Had lunch with the American Consul yesterday. He is a stuffy egg but a nice guy when he starts to talk. Went over to Edith Gentil's house and heard that same stuff of Brazilian girls absorbing all the U.S.A. culture, like movies, records, and boogy-woogy. Group of U.S. Army Transport planes came over yesterday - they looked nice flying in formation. I watched them trying to launch some *jangadas* [fishing rafts] the other day and they looked very picturesque. Even Orson Welles could not screw that up.

March 10, 1943

The three days of carnival is not the time to be in any city for a short time, especially here in Fortaleza as this is a nice town but I am at the moment at the country club. I remember that night in Illinois, when I worked at country club, Bill and I walked to the Tavern from the Club and got a few beers and sang a few marching songs and got chills thinking if we would ever be doing this for real. The shower at the hotel Fortaleza. I always meant to fix that up. The ups and downs of this new job. I don't know if I am going to like it or not.

The Americans I meet are always going through time. They are fresh out of the States. The time I sat in the Panair do Brasil [airline] waiting room and saw the plane from Miami come in with two pretty girls. The sergeant and I were talking about how nice and light and they looked.

No paint, no beauty marks just nice and fresh and healthy looking. They probably took me for a native.

The pleasant flatness of the town which reminds you somewhat of a Midwestern U.S.A. town. The kids yelling curses in English when you don't give them money. The people selling lace blouses to a couple of tough army corporals when the army corps was buying hammocks.

March 12, 1943

With a Curtiss P-40 Warhawk in Fortaleza.

Time flies but I wonder how fast. More and more this seems not to be the job for me. What was needed here was an administrative officer. One who was good at details and could handle office routine; now they have Jordan Young and I think everyone around here is disgusted. I will still stay with my original 3 months proposition but I am going to mark off days. I arrived here March 4th and it is the 12th already – almost two weeks gone. Krug, the big boss, arrives today and the cleaning and straightening up is terrific. I will probably learn a lot from this office work if I live through it. Guess I can't be a short snorter until I cross an ocean by plane. Meeting all sort of aviators and people and stuff. I am thinking seriously about the army stuff again. Maybe I can go to officers training school or something. Nine days gone - 81 more days.

March 16, 1943

Had supper Saturday night at the Jangada Club. It was nice but other than witty speech in Portuguese by the President of the organization and a pedantic speech by our chief the thing was rather dull. I have been busy as a busy bee here (stinks) writing this report and something is welling up in my chest that does not bode well for the future. Was offered a job last night.

March 17, 1943

This morning as I was taking a shower I realized what had happened more or less to me. When I was living in São Paulo, I had sort of settled down. I had become as they say in Portuguese "ambientado" - I was in the environment. I had a bicycle and dropped over to people whenever I went cycling and had a glass of milk and cookies and then went out for supper. House and square dancing and all fell into a nice pattern there. That all made up a balanced life. I did not it like it at the time but now that I am up here in Fortaleza I can see how nice it was.

I am not happy here because the work is something I am not suited for. The training I will get will no doubt be valuable in the long run but in this day and age I think it is folly for you to hang around offices getting training when there are such interesting jobs to be done, especially in Brazil. It always takes a certain length of time for the fact to sink into my head that you can't just enter a city and swing into all the social life of a town without first going through a rough bumpy period where you stay home and go to sleep and dream about the ---- and stuff. Well, whatever I do I must move out to the beach and get myself a nice room and enjoy the comforts of swimming and the pleasant sights of Jangadas beneath the palm trees.

I was made transportation chief among the other things that I am doing here. With no subsequent raise in pay. Funny when you live in a town like this I realize the importance of contacting the Brazilians and living with the Brazilian families. Yet I don't do it. Saturday afternoon went swimming with Dr. Zuckerman and Col. Driesback. I saw how nice it was on the beach with the fishermen coming off the jangadas and cleaning and dividing the fish on the beach. The warmness of the ocean water impressed me. I met Dick Dyer[33] from AP who is up here doing a story. I get real griped when I know I could be doing could be doing the same thing more or less. McCortney from TIME magazine is coming up also with a photographer to cover the story.

March 22, 1943

Just to prove to myself that time flies I thought I'd just knock off a few minutes and try and write a few words on the present situation. I still haven't resolved my problem but the doc (Dr. Zuckerman) who at first didn't care when I went now wants me to stay because I might become an administrative officer but I still it stinks on ice.

March 23, 1943

I think perhaps some of my difficulties with Brazilian people are due to my being frank and sincere upon meeting a person. That is, I warm up very fast and do not like this vast playing around period where you must get to know people before you can be friendly. If I like a person I get friendly and stay friendly until they do something that makes me change my mind but I believe their system is too cold and calculating. I think this agriculture professor here helped clear up a point. This is not the time for me to spend in an office trying to build up knowledge as an office manager type of stuff. It is too easy to fall into a rut. One has to fight against this office boy personality that you develop doing all sorts of odd jobs and no specific ones.

I will speak to Dr. Wagley when he returns. Dr. Crist, a professor I had for geography in my first semester at Illinois, is in Bahia working for Rubber Reserve. They have a very bad policy here in employment. Anyone who is hired down here gets a very low salary in comparison to those hired in Washington. Instead of sending those who know a little about the country back to Washington to help any program they continually send down new men who do not speak the language. These men employ us guys for interpreters and we then have to do the work of an efficient secretary in the states. Except here it is in two languages. Shoemaker left for Recife and Mr. Finner moved into his place. I still feel I would like to move out from the hotel. Funny that even though I am

---

33 Richard Dyer worked for the AP from 1940-42. Afterwards he moved to Costa Rica to work as a publicist for the United Fruit Company. In his later years he was the publisher of The Tico Times, Costa Rica's English language weekly newspaper.

making $100 a month my living expenses seem to be eating it all up. When I received $25 bucks a month I had more money. I sent a check home the other day - my first!

March 24, 1943

Yesterday was an ordinary day. Went to the airport in the morning to try and get the doctor off to Belém but not until Friday. Spoke to Captain Lynch and then came back to office. Sat around waiting for something to do and got nice and disgusted until lunch time. Then I had lunch at my grand Palace Hotel. Back to work at 1:30 and picked up a secretary for Mr. Fleming.

Also talked (battled) with Lt. Van Buren and got a suit for him that he thought he was buying for 15 dollars and it turned out to be 50 dollars. Senhor Young had to arbitrate. Got it down to 45 bucks but the strain on me was terrific. Then both turned out to be gentlemen and Masons and all was forgiven.

We went to the airport again and one of our men was going through from Rio to Belém - a sanitary engineer from Georgia. In the evening I had a lousy supper and walked around the park and then to bed by 9:30. I suppose I could make a simple day like this one sound very intriguing and exciting but I see no necessity or desire to do so. I am making up mind to fight against this office job.

March 25, 1943

Yesterday seems like Sunday and was typical of Brazilian indulgence in holidays to stop work and enjoy life. It is the anniversary of the abolition of slavery here in the state of Ceará, an act which took place before the rest of Brazil.

I went out to the airport and got two doctors off to Belém on an ATC [Air Transport Command] plane. We arrived at PICEY (the name of the airport) this morning and then didn't leave until 1 pm. Spent the morning at the field and met a corporal who was at Champaign, Illinois the same time I was. We chewed the fat and funny you forget names that you have not thought of for year or so.

Saw a bomber came in; when it got about 15-50 feet from the ground the pilot saw that only one wheel had come down. The boys tore down the run way on a jeep with fire extinguishers but they saw it and zoomed up. Worked on it until the wheel came down. They landed, had a bite to eat, and then flew on to Natal and east to north Africa, the Ascension Islands, and then Dakar. Next there was the navy shuttle plane and then army transport, which was an old Eastern airlines ship and pilot. Boy the way that guy banked the plane on the side of the field was terrific; those guys come in on a dime and ten cents change.

We had lunch at the field helping to inaugurate their new mess. The consul, Capt. Van Buren, Zuckerman, and Franny were among the people who sat at my table. Fried chicken, green peas - everything was terrific.

In the afternoon we went to the beach and I took a movie of a few jangadas coming in. It is wonderful at the beach really. While we were there we met an RAF [U.K. Royal Air Force] pilot whose plane had been temporarily disabled here. They are funny looking jobs with big under slung bellies to help them fly direct from Natal to Bathurst about 1400 miles. Once you get to talking with these English boys you find them very nice and interesting. If ever there will be a rapprochement made between England and the U.S. there will be power unlimited.

At the hotel earlier when we had got back from the field a few P-38's[34] flew over so damn low that it woke everyone up in this sleepy town. We walked on the beach at night before we went home and had supper at the hotel. The band played in the park at night and we saw two American aviators making passes at some girls. There was sort of an argument and one of the boys had to call up Capt. Zuckerman to stitch up his forehead about 11 o'clock at night.

Wagley comes back from his tour and guess I'll have to talk to him this week before he leaves. I like it here and all the baloney but I want to see the interior of this country – to hell with the cities.

A Long Digression on Jangadas

Fisherman and their *jangadas* dotted the beaches. *Jangadas* were (and still are) rafts made of five or six wooden logs that are lashed together, with a huge triangular sail along with some very rudimentary fishing equipment, as well as a little stool, a basket for the fish, and a centerboard. There was a raised bar across the bottom where the mast could be slotted in to catch the wind shifts. The logs of which the boats are constructed came from the southern state of Rio Grande do Sul and were shipped up on the old four-mast fishing schooners. During the war years there was a scarcity of these logs and the price of *jangadas* went way up; they cost fifty dollars when I was there.

---

[34] Lockheed P-38 Lightning.

The fishermen were part of a fleet and would go out for to sea for days. The *jangadeiros* who manned the *jangadas* were the color of mahogany. Their primitive way of life revolved around the sea and they had not changed their ways for many years. Living in the "second block" of the beach of Iracema, they lived a rustic life in homes nestled within palm trees and constructed of materials found on the beach.

Their distinctive fishing boats were found only in the Northeast of Brazil and most commonly in the state of Ceará. The boats usually contained a crew of four men, but smaller, two-man craft were also common. While it was said that four logs are usually the width of a *jangada*, there were variations.

Each man on the *jangada* had a particular role. The *mestre* was the boat's owner or, if the owner did not sail, the captain. The other crewmen were subordinate to this man, who was generally older and considered the best sailor with knowledge of the wind, etc. The *proeira* was the man who stayed in front of the boat and helped with the sails. The two other crew members were the *bico de proa* and *rebique*. The *rebique* was also the word for the front part of the *jangada* that got pointed when the prow hit water. The man in this position brought the clubs for beating the fish during the "little wind" season, and the coal and pots during the harvest.

Every crew member had a specific job to do when the *jangada* was in the water and when they reached the fishing grounds and stopped to fish. Their jobs depended upon the seasons of the year.

Jangada rafts and the jangadeiros who fished from them on the beach at Fortaleza.

"*Tempo de ir e vir,*" which literally means the time of coming and going of little wind, was the part of the year when a trip would be a one-day affair. During this time the men had to bring food with them. The *mestre* did not bring anything but the boat. During the *safra*, or harvest season, the men went out three times a week, leaving early one day and returning the morning of the following day. The *proeira leva a quirmanga* was a sort of small wooden barrel with food in it. During a trip of little wind, all the food was taken in a dry condition so nothing had to be cooked on board, as was commonly the practice during the harvest season.

The *mestre* had the *pinambaba*, an apparatus that had complete fishing tackle with hooks and weights. As they were caught, the fish were marked to identify who caught it - some by nicking the tail; others by a cross on the belly. When the men returned to shore after a night on the high seas, they divided the fish up in to three parts: half went to the *mestre* if he was the owner of the *jangada* and the rest was divided up equally among the other three men. If the men were on a boat that did not belong to them then half went to the owner of the *jangada* and the rest was divided equally among the four crew members. The price of fish in Fortaleza was rather high considering the abundance of the product. I never bought any of the daily catch as I was allergic to fish.

There was a certain art to the building of these boats and only fishermen could legally be the owners. In a vague sense of the word, there existed a fishermen's guild on the beach of Iracema headed by Jerônimo Andre de Souza. Most of the men who fished did not own their boats because of the expense, and it was rare to find as many as two or three boats in the possession of one man. The *jangadas* were divided up into unions, identified on the sails by the letters Z1, Z2, or Z3. These men did not land at any beach but their own.

Groups of boys handled the logs upon which they rolled the ship up to high and dry land. The men wore straw hats painted with some sort of white pigment. Their clothing was mostly black leather, which they seemed to prefer, and they went without shoes.

In the time of the little wind, the men went out to sea five times a week, resting on Sunday and most of the time on Thursday to repair the *jangadas*. The food that they generally took included meat, bread, *frango* (fried chicken), *rapadura* (cane sugar), and bananas.

Sunset postcard entitled *"Entardecer no Rio Potengy, Natal."*

Jangadeiros I Knew

I visited and talked to a *jangadeiro* named Raimundo Correia Lima, called Tatá. His home was near the beach, the so-called second block off the beach. Tatá and Jerônimo were two of the *jangadeiros* who made a famous *jangada* trip to Rio de Janeiro, 1,650 miles over open ocean, to made demands of President Vargas regarding bad working conditions.

Tatá was ill at the time I visited him but showed a lively interest in the economic and social side of fishing. He was disturbed by the lack of legislation regarding the fishermen, in particular the promise of land that was never given to them. Tatá seemed to be part Indian, whereas his wife had black features. He was illiterate but his wife was not. He spoke knowingly of the difference in the wage scale between his country and the U.S.A. He spoke with pride about the *jangadeiros.* The problem was he spoke a jargon that I and the Brazilian lady who accompanied me had trouble understanding.

Jerônimo took me out on his boat alone one day. The vast ocean and this simple raft defied any logical definition, and I was so scared I just grabbed the main mast and held on for dear life. When we returned to land we had to catch the waves coming in and follow them to the shore, like a surfer.

Orson Welles and the Jangadeiros

Nelson Rockefeller, the director of the Institute of Inter-American Affairs asked the famous American film director Orson Welles to make a movie about Latin America as part of Pres. Roosevelt's "Good Neighbor Policy." Part of the film was to tell the story of the *jangadeiros'* trip to Rio to protest their dangerous working conditions. Welles went to Fortaleza and filmed several of the *jangadeiros*, including Jerônimo and Tatá, but the film, to be entitled "It's All True," was never finished.[35]

Jean Manzon was a colorful French cameraman and director who worked with Orson Welles on the movie. Manzon had me thrown out of a conference organized by Sumner Welles in Rio because I was annoying him. I saw him filming in Fortaleza:

> March 27, 1943
>
> Yesterday I had an odd experience of being in a good mood of don't push people around when you can't tell where they are heading. Jean something or other [Manzon], the French photographer who had Paul and I thrown out of that conference room. He filmed the retreat at Dunkirk and was filming in the Spanish Civil War.
>
> The flying officer that got his head bashed in when he went to a garden and had some beer and the girls flocked around him and one Brazilian got angry and swung a chair. The boys were sober and walked out instead of starting a riot. But result was all transient officers must stay on base. Those boys in the P-38's have such a short time to enjoy their rank. The doc was very sympathetic - but it is always the men that go through that cause all the trouble. The big battle in Belém when the boys of a troop ship got drunk in the district and invaded a private home and raped a girl and tore the house apart. The Brazilian troops with bayonets in their guns herded the soldiers up even to the point of having machine guns ready. No soldiers were seen in the streets for a long time after that.
>
> We had an opportunity to see a typical night before 400 men left for the Amazon Valley to work in Rubber Plantations. They were playing some native tunes and men at a distance were shuffling about in a sort of dance. It was the first time I saw men dancing with men.

---

[35] A book titled *It's All True, Orson Welles' Pan-American Odessey*, by Catherine L. Bernamou, describes the making of the film, while a documentary on Welles' project under the same name, containing the footage from the *jangadeiro* film, was released in 1993

Consulate workers and Jordan watching the departure of rubber workers.

I am afraid that I could never swallow that pioneer angle thought that they are giving those men. I cannot picture pioneers in uniform, being marched into a certain region with a guarantee as to how much they are going to make and how much they will send to the folks back home. I often wonder - while watching these men - at what point individualism is a healthy and democratic sign; that is, there is a point where this Latin, not excitable or super rigid in anything, is good or bad. As I saw these men climbing today heading for the Amazon, I had to laugh at the thought of Hitler or any dictator trying to make an exacting group out of them. Maybe it could be done but the spirit would be entirely changed.

I was forcibly impressed by a woman doing social work. She was at the Prado at ten o'clock at night, working away lining men up and giving a calm word here and there and then at 6 a.m. the next morning when we got to the camp today she was there already. I would like to do a story on her in an American magazine as she is a very interesting person.

The men going up into the trucks looked more scared then anything else but they lightened and went out to cheers of the on lookers. When the final speech was made 3 workers were worried when he mentioned the battle of rubber; the social worker was afraid they would interpret this that they were going to fight in a real war. The whispering campaign by the Integralists[36] and Fascists has been pretty strong; after we left last night they picked up a scuzzy German who was loitering around the camp at 1 a.m.

Jean Manzon got some good shots yesterday. I helped Franny out again and got my picture in the paper when he was interviewed. I served as an interpreter.

Oh yes, I received a letter from Rio stating that I had been with the organization a few months and that I was not entitled to a living allowance but my work was satisfactory and then at the end of six months on June 1st I would upon recommendation be reclassified with a raise. I don't know. I'm still afraid of this rut business. The job offer with ADP still holds. Those damn P3-8's came over again with a real boom and sacred the hell out of everyone in town.

March 29, 1943

I guess I skipped over Saturday and Sunday and will try to remember what happened. I can only think now of how angry you get at the sight of all that gasoline being flagrantly wasted here in Fortaleza with the great crisis in the U.S., pleasure cars & taxis - everyone has gas.

Saturday afternoon went out to the beach with Jean Manzon and met some of the jangada men with whom he had worked during the Orson Welles filming here. Jerônimo, the leader of the jangadeiros here, was one of them men who took the jangadas down to Rio. The man that died during the filming of the picture was drunk and fell off the jangada and drowned.

These men have a sort of union and a chief to represent them in problems etc. We had a drink of some cachaça [sugar cane liquor] and then a nice little chaser to get rid of the taste.

The boys that roll the boats up to the beach get one mil réis a boat.

Saturday evening I took Marinha to the movies and it was damn good. Took a walk to her house and a cab home. Had lunch Sunday at the airport again with the soldiers. Damn good food; still got diarrhea though. Still plan to move out to the beach. Had a refreshing talk with Finney; saw how an ordinary American reacts to certain things I have become accustomed to down here. Will complete the details later.

Stuck in Fortaleza

March 30, 1943

---

[36] Brazilian fascist organization in the 30's and 40's, also called "Greenshirts." I later met an *integralista*, Dom Helder Camara, in 1966 (see Chapter 16)

The little things in life here go to make up dreams. Funny how walking home from work last night there was a prostitute leaning against the lamp post. In the shadow of a house entrance was a beggar. They were both eyeing each other. Along the street to the hotel are a number of these dance hall types of whorehouses. They are up on the second floor and have an orchestra blaring forth. The men are usually clustered in small knots in front of the entrances. Later at night you see all colors of women walking down the streets.

Sherry and I walked down a corridor with a lot of rooms on it. A woman raised her skirt to her waist and beckoned to him; he let fly with an oh boy, and we decided to go home instead. Doc here estimates more than 90% of them diseased. Sherry and Frank went up again and began to bargain with them and found they came down to 15 mil réis, which was 75 cents.

It all seems rather sordid to me and I haven't been near one of these places since November in São Paulo. Sex is something I still can't get pegged down one way or the other in my mind. I'll easily admit that as Americans, we are hypocrites on the subject and can't see the point of view that the Latins hold or as a matter of fact, the view held by the city people of the U.S. O Hell. I don't agree with anyone.

Worked last night until 12 o'clock in the stock room and enjoyed it. Meyers, the accountant from Rio now working in Belém, came in and told me about [Paul] Oechsli (my roommate from São Paulo).

Nothing special during the day. Took Dyer to the airport and did not eat lunch there. The navy plane was packed with mica and quartz stuff so there was no place for any passengers. Usually, the fellows told me, all north bound planes are empty. I could get a ride to Africa but I could not get back so I would have to keep on going until I reached Chunking China – same idea and it isn't really working either.

Sometime I want to develop as an idea that smells and odors and clothing and the way people look and how they live up in front of the movies and Sunday night differs so drastically on other days. I also want to explore how the boys here don't stare at the girls the way they do in the south of Brazil. The funny pajama like clothing the natives seem to wear. The fresh steady ocean trade winds that always make you feel good to be alive. The patient, inquisitive looks that are always directed at the stranger, be he or she national or foreign. The taste of that sharp sea smell that you get as soon as you reach the Rio sea front. The solders drilling front of the hotel. The people seem what you would call back home nondescript. You do get those sudden squalls of rain, fierce almost solid sheets of water that fall for about 5 or ten minutes and then disappear.

Though I am still all messed up inside I feel good for some unknown reason. The bill at the hotel cost 50 bucks for the room, etc. But am moving today for the beach and feel good about it.

Yesterday was out at airport again trying to get passage for five doctors on Thursday. OK I think. Funny I caught short wave from U.S.A. last night and the most popular song is from Brazil –wow does it stink in this jazzed up version.

Sr. Edwards is driving me nuts with those poems but it is a pleasant diversion. There is a lot to this place or any place that must be dug up and reconstructed with words to make it live and breathe.

Lt. Wadsworth, naval attaché, came over last night and we showed him our Lab. He seems to be of the mould set type of young man from Yale and with a little continental background but as enthusiastic as a dead fish.

Watched Manzon take pictures of the Prado camp and was impressed at how he does his work.

I must study more Portuguese.

April 1, 1943

Don't feel good – phooey – I got angry the other day when one of the young kids who was working as a messenger in our office got fired because his name was Wolfgang Steindoffer. No other reason mind you but the fact of his name. He was born in Brazil of Austrian parents. I guess it is what you call a sign of times. I went on record as against it.

Moved out to the beach last night and think it will be very nice there even if I moved in bass-ackwards. I think or rather the thought came to me yesterday that I will mature very slowly as this is my nature but I think I will stay young longer this way. I dunno. I'm not worried about it in the least. I don't give damn for position or much else.

April 2, 1943

It's a damned shame the way I have to lug those docs out to the airport and back again when they don't succeed in getting an army transport plane. I have had Burgos out there two weeks.

Had fun last night - maybe I have grown to like Marinha because when Willy showed up and began to pitch it at her he threw it plenty along and made some hits. Funny I didn't give it a second thought but what the hell.

Bullet holes in the back yard and the Padre - funny world. Meyers sleeps in a hammock. I sleep in the bed. Raining like hell here for the last three or four days. If this keeps up no drought victims but flood victims. Wagley is going on a trip. Zuckerman is going on a trip. Everyone is going on a trip except Young. Phooey!!

April 5, 1943

Feel like I am in a rut again. Very interesting where I am living - odd getting up at night and finding a woman standing beside your bed and putting flowers in your hair. Very interesting. But I think I don't like it doesn't fit in with my plans of life etc. The damn fool who almost got electrocuted this morning because of the short in the refrigerator. It is odd how these things that are romantic up to a certain point get so God awful dull and uninteresting after a time.

Odd about that B-20 bomber who got lost half way across the Atlantic on the way to Africa and ended here in Fortaleza wondering if he was in Africa or not.

What in the hell happened to this morning - it is just zipping by and I can't get my fingers into it. I must fire some cooks today and don't feel too good about it. Must call up Gordon. The girl in my room startled me last night but I hope we can put an end to it because it isn't nice and gives the house a bad name. The dinner at the Jangada Club was all right but until you get into those people they seem to be a bunch of block headed fools. The English club afterwards was not much different but may be I was on the defensive. How the hell those fellows manage to go whoring and drinking every night and then get up the next morning with an o.k. look in their eyes. I am in the mood to quit right now. Every God damned person in the office is taking trips except Young. Bull***!!

April 7, 1943

Never a dull moment at our house. Last night around 2 o'clock we were pleasantly awakened by a few nude pretty women sitting on my bed and quite a riot afterwards but I succeeded in getting them all off and out of the house. Damn I am going to catch a cold if I wrestle on the floor any more with naked women. But no one was the worse for the interlude and no screwing took place. I almost broke my arm when I fell on the floor with that babe on top of me.

April 8, 1943

You know I could settle down here but am afraid of the idea. Got a letter from Ruth the other day and she seems to have changed a bit. I can't put my finger on it but there is change. Golly with all these airplanes I am meeting and stuff I'm afraid I will get blasé about airplanes. The airplane of CAF (China Air Force) comes through here. Also many of the men have made the trip so many times they don't think anything of it. Some Englishmen got off his ship the other day and we got into a conversation about the Tunisian battle front. It turned out he had just left the combat region two days ago; it was all rather personal.

Golly but it is raining here. I don't see how we can continue to have work when it rains so. I don't write about the war usually because it has become such a part of you that you take it for granted like the weather. That I realize is an unfortunate position because there is so much anguish and suffering going on.

The British are now bombing Berlin and the newspapers gloat that the raids are heavier than those ever visited on London. The Germans shout they have exterminated all the Jews in Poland, etc., etc. In Africa it seems we may even defeat Rommel's forces. In Europe, the RAF & American bombers continue their pounding of Germany but I don't see why Germany should fall if Madrid. London or any other city did not fall from attacks from the air that was not followed up by a ground attack. The Germans in Russia are fighting a defensive retreat action after two years of success. The Japs are still taking the measure of the Americans on the whole but losing in small individual encounters.

It is odd but most of the U.S. I believe think that the Germans as something we can take the measure of but the Japs are another sort of animal that is not clear yet. The soft pleasure loving Americans certainly disappeared fast in the battle zone.

April 14, 1943

It is funny how you can't get a historical perspective of a place like Fortaleza. Now and then you can see the ruins of the old Dutch fort along the coast; unfortunately the cannons are now resting in front of the Jangada Club. Rusty puny things that they fire crackers from it at every dinner. We know that in Juazeiro [do Norte, a nearly town] there was a priest called Padre Cicero[37] who in 1914 raised the people in revolt against something or other. I will try and read some archives on this stuff.

I have decided to move my house again after boys came home drunk again last night and wrecked the house in part. I also requested a change of project but I have my fingers crossed. I am moving to a pensão on the beach with him. I am learning that the word pensão has another meaning here in the north of Brazil.

---

[37] Cícero Romão Batista, a Catholic priest whose life as a community leader in Juazeiro do Norte, has inspired a huge cult following in the Northeast of Brazil.

April 15, 1943

Just what in the hell do I have to do now that the monthly summaries are being typed and the doctor's relatórios are all o.k. Phooey. Nuts.

It is possible that it is not that the Cearaense are better workers but that their level of life has been so low that they live on a lot less than other people therefore they are wanted all over Brazil – but they are nevertheless popular in the other parts of the Amazon Territory (the Acre territory). Wherever they went because they were starving or pioneering spirit is another thing. There does not exist in Brazil - especially among the common people - the factors that go to developing a drive or a force to make these people go into unexplored regions of the world. It does not exist here. That effort for self betterment toward a better life doesn't exist either. That great common denominator in the U.S.A. does constitute a force in Brazil.

You can exist here is tropical countries while in the temperate countries you would die during the winter season. These people may be strong - considering the environment, considering the climate, and considering the food they get - but I am beginning to wonder what - ????? As I am writing this a little kid, about 5 years old, is standing outside the gate saying "Senhor, da me um pedaço de pão" – please give me piece of bread. He repeats this over and over again. God how many lives are broken here before they are even born into thinking that families like ours did live in Hoovertowns in little huts but God I do not remember the begging like this.

April 18, 1943

Been taking a beating these last few days. It is better that it happened now than later. First, I was ticked off by the FBI man about making myself at home in other people's houses. I guess I had to learn sometime but I always expect people without question to share what they have and sort of the same with other people but you can't do that. Other people have different ideas about the property sense and resent other's usurping this. Must see if I can learn this lesson.

The other is I am losing a splendid opportunity to assume responsibility. I have plenty of work here I want to get it. I just must mold my character to it. I have decided that I am mentally lazy and unless stirred well I do not do not go out of my way to impress people. There is a lot of work ahead of me in all these fields and it is good that I can see these things now at this age and under these circumstances rather than much later. Keep your fingers crossed and watch your step Young because you are now molding the future. The clay is in your hands and you can make anything from a spit ball to a successful and useful object if it.

April 21, 1943

Am in front of the Prado camp trying to find one of our doctors. Everyone o.k. This will be a trip of 260 kilometers where we will be visiting towns like Sobral and Tiangua in a station wagon with plenty of people.

I am writing this 1 hour and 15 minutes from Fortaleza. There is a funny dried up river here and it is 163 kilometers to Sobral. Had coffee - a nice little set up in the open air with plenty of Carnauba palm trees. The roads are good because there were no cattle or cars on them. Lot of begging; if they spent half as much time working as they did begging they might have a lot more money. The mountains in the distance form a nice a picture like the fringe of a picture ... the little town of Riachuelo comes round the bend in the road ... two girls taking a bath in the river. We are in some nice little typical small town stuff where a guy is in store complaining about the last corn meal that he bought and the circle of listeners and the little goats running through the streets.

Little clumps of mountains come and go. Had a good lunch in Hotel Cearense, a small little town of 200 population. Paid three bucks and had meals for 75 cents and people friendly and had a bottle of beer.

Received 1200 cruzierios or 60 bucks part of my pay check. I gave 25 to Barbosa, then I sent to Paul –35 dollars to room rent. This was the April 1st check 28 mil réis for groceries, 104 mil for films.

April 28, 1943

It seems the plateau period has again set in my diary writing. Have had a tough time writing. Moved to the boarding house. OK except for the flies. The food is fair.

Been wolfing around for a job with ADP [Airport Development Program]. I don't know but it seems to be within the realm of possibility - 300 to 350 dollars a month. A good story is the C.O. and the prostitutes. The law here in Fortaleza and the two that almost got arrested - then he himself downtown. The ships, five of them, riding with their lights on – hope to hell they don't get picked off. The dummies.

Capt. Zuckerman became Major Zuckerman - duly celebrated. It seems the more letters I write the less I receive. A country by the name of Soviet Russia broke relations with a gov't in exile called Poland. This sure has screwed things up in the field of world affairs.

There is one thing that I seem to forget. All these men with whom I am associating are directors of projects with experience and background here and I am disagreeing and opening my trap when I should not be doing it. And I see also that I have forgotten something that I thought guided my actions but I see was not as strong as I thought it was: the myth that I would be happy at a good steady job. That would not make a millionaire. I don't think this present work is just what I wanted but it shows how restless I can get. I am sitting now in an automobile in front of Wagley's house waiting for them to finish breakfast. A lot of ships in the harbor and while I was swimming another came in. I think today will be an interesting day for me.

April 29, 1943

I guess I was right about being an interesting day for me. I received a wage increase of about 70 bucks a month and it left me strangely cool. I found out that no job existed at the wages I wanted. Well what the hell I asked for 300 a month and at 22 that's a lot of dough. I guess the 50 I am getting is lot - considering my 22 years of age it is terrific especially for my first real job.

April 30, 1943

12 mil réis for candy
62 mil for stamps
10 mil for taxi
400 mil for rent for house
20 mil oranges
90 mil mosquito net
5 mil laundry
300 mil horse

May 13, 1943

I guess I really have been slipping. I don't write worth a damn - but I am being sent to Belém soon and have been in communication with Oechsli (São Paulo roommate). This is the morning of May 13. I am once more resolving to keep this damn thing up to date. The many interesting and informative tidbits are escaping me.

For example I am in the midst of a funny little thing that could be called a romance yet it is not a romance. Funny I can't figure it out. I don't love the girl and she is fraught with all complexes that surround Latin girls. We stayed two nights just talking away and hell I just can't figure it out. She said she doesn't love me.

I have also spent some time with the *jangadeiros* and the "*tempo de e ir e vir.*" They use this expression when they go and come back the same day. They take prepared food and go as far as the "wall" where the wind fails and they come back. No wind - that that is why they go and come back that same day.

Funny item I found yesterday about Senta[38] paying 5 contos a month to all the papers for publicity. Again I only heard this and cannot vouch for its authenticity.

Had lunch with a girl from Senta and in general the last few days have been a swell time. I like Fortaleza a lot and went out in a jangada the other day and enjoyed myself a lot. The wallop that the boat receives really knocks the hell out of you unless you are ready for it.

---

38 "Senta a pua" ("Fight with spurs!") was the motto of the Brazilian Fighter Squadron, so this reference might be to that squadron.

Chapter 7. The Meeting in Belém (May 1943)

News began to come in that the Amazon project was not performing well in their monthly reports and they badly needed someone further north. I was sent to Belém for brief trip and to scope out the problem. I spent only 15 days in Belém on this trip but it changed my life 10 years later.

Arriving in Belém

The half hour drive to Belém was like rolling back history. Cities have a feel to them, and this one was like diving into something warm, pulsating, and enveloping. What a sleepy town Belém was, more Portuguese than anything else I'd seen in Brazil. It was different from Rio de Janeiro or São Paulo. In those cities I felt right at home; they were cosmopolitan European cities similar to the USA except that everyone was speaking Portuguese. But Belém was different.

I was lodged in the Hotel Central, an old run down hotel that had a good kitchen. I remember the morning ritual well. We got up at 6 am while it was still cool and had breakfast on *mamão* (very sweet papaya) and other tropical fruits and then would walk to work. The sun would just be hitting the dome of the old cathedral as I arrived at my office. There I was met by the project's director, Dr. Kenneth Chamberlain Waddell, an MD and old Amazon hand.[39] He tried to teach the young American Lieutenants about the river but they could not grasp the vastness of the Amazon.

May 18, 1943

Flew here on Air Transport Command, an old Eastern Airlines plane. The trip took me about 1,000 miles from Fortaleza. We landed at São Luis [capitol of the state of Maranhão]. The men are not army but old Eastern Airlines pilots. We sat in funny metal seats along the side of the ship and found them uncomfortable... this is one of those times of mind over matter.

I feel dog tired but a recapitulation of the trip is necessary. Yesterday I left Fortaleza on an Air Transport Command plane. These are old, I think, DC 3's and were part of the Silver Fleet of the Eastern Air Lines. The seats are all out and you sit on the side in little inverted steel plates. It is not important but what do you want for nothing. The cargo is all strapped down in the middle. It felt funny at the airport with all the soldiers joking and saying goodbye.

I met Dr. Dantas on the plane and also Dr. Arlan. You often lose perspective but when you figure that I went about 1000 miles without a stop from 1:30 to 5:30 that is not bad traveling. We hit one decent air pocket. Hit my seat with a klunk. The São Luis stopover was uneventful except it is odd to see American soldiers at all these airfields wherever you stop. We let off some unfortunate sailor and took off in ten minutes. After we left São Luis, the capital of the state of Maranhão, the terrain really looked like jungle - all thick trees out there. The assistant on the plane, I suppose he had been a steward before, came out and talked to us saying the jungle was really fierce and I wouldn't want to stay more than one night in it. About 5:30 pm sighted Belém and golly it seems to be a super airfield loaded with all sort of airplanes. They are all shapes and sizes that you can easily get killed walking carelessly.

I went into town with the Panair pilots and stopped at the Grand Hotel. We then went to a French restaurant and had wonderful food and stayed overnight. Funny U.S. money accepted here as legal tender there is so much of it around.

Saw Paul[40] my ex roommate that evening.

---

[39] Dr. Waddell worked for years at Henry Ford's failed rubber plantations on the Tapajos River, up the Amazon from Belém.

[40] Paul was the American student I became friendly with in São Paulo and had offered to share his *pensão* room with me. He had a Rotary scholarship and like myself was trapped in Brazil at the beginning of the war. Paul, however, was a certified conscientious objector. I

Next morning saw Wagner and he requested that I help on the Food and Nutrition for the new Curry Hospital and there seems to be a lot of mismanagement here and I had better keep my mouth shut and my eyes open. Something I am not good at. I am at the mouth of the Amazon and not enthusiastic – Poosha Vida[41] I am getting Mole.

Paul Oechsli was employed by the Coordinator of the Inter-American Affairs, Food and Nutrition Division (affectionately called the Fruit and Nuts division) while I was attached to the Health and Sanitation Division.

May 19, 1943

After one day at the camp at Tapaná, I have really lost my girlish laughter. Of all our SESP camps, this one seems to be the worst. Organize your report to cover the physical conditions, then the set up of the docs, etc. – then the men in the camp where they are from, why they want to go and where, how much, etc., are they happy...

If the work of the SESP projects per contracts signed between them and SAVA[42] SEMTA[43] for medical inspection and treatment of workers, sanitation of the camps and barracks inspection, and the O.K.'ing of the food supply, there is no evidence of this work being done at the Belém Tapaná Camp worthy of mention.

The Belém Tapaná camp is located 14 miles outside of the city of Belém on the margin of the River Pará. Originally built for about 1500 men the camp has been continually enlarged until the present day capacity is near 4000. The number of migrants in camp at the present moment is near 3000. The camp is surrounded by a wire fence and at the main entrance are some armed guards who loll about the gate but do not pay much attention to anyone. The camp seems to give an appearance with about 5 streets of wooden barracks, which are about ¼ of a mile from the gate in the direction of the river. As you approach the camp there is evidence of plant cultivation - many acres of land in cooperation with Food and Nutrition and SWI.

The SESP hospital is located in an ex-xarque [meat drying facility] factory and has accommodations for about 30 beds, one isolation ward (which

---

have always had a warn spot on my heart for the Rotary scholarship people as his scholarship supported two people.

41 "*Puxa vida,* meaning "Holy cow!" or "Wow!"

42 *Superintendência para o Abastecimento do Vale da Amazônia* (Superintendency for the Provisioning of the Amazon Valley, or SAVA) of the Brazilian government.

43 *Serviço Especial de Mobilização de Trabalhadores para a Amazônia* (Special Service of Mobilization of Workers for the Amazon, or SEMTA).

> is badly guarded), and one section in a huge central room for bronchitis and respiratory diseases. There are three doctors - Benting, Amorim, and Oseas - working here. They are assisted by 20 nurses.
>
> There are three toilets in the hospital; they were usually not working when I visited the hospital. The men were sanitary guards but there was no security in the hospital nor was there any mosquito netting for the malaria cases.
>
> There were two interns in the main ward theoretically guarded by men to prevent strangers from entering and leaving the hospital. The floors of the hospital are continually swept but there are a considerable number of flies which constantly covered the beds of the patients. Flit is sprayed twice a day and naturally does not have much effect. It has a small hospital kitchen that is in the process of remodeling but is not at present completed. This will serve food for the patients who at the present get three meals a day from the administration building kitchen which is different from the SEMTA workers' general kitchen.
>
> Behind the hospital about 50 feet of land slopes down to the river where most of the drainage goes. This does not constitute a problem here because the men use it as privy and it is the only sanitary facility excepting the hospital. There is a little pier to the left where the men disembark from the boats.
>
> Off color story about the guy who had his hammock in his hotel room in the Acre region of the Amazon. The gentleman in the other bedroom had his hammock hitched to the same post. But as luck would have it the gentleman in the other room also was entertaining some woman. As he banged away at her the hammock jumped and pulled the post every which way. And he had to lay in his hammock and grin and bear it.

There was one good restaurant in the place called Madame Garay's. The Madame in question was French and catered to Pan American pilots and the high brass at the airport. There was another place that didn't have any air conditioning, as Madame Garay's did. We called it the "*borraco quente*", or "hot hole", in contrast to the air-conditioned "*borraco frio*" or "cold hole." We liked the hot hole better because the beer tasted colder there.

The City of Belém

The warmth and lushness of the town took me over. There was a softness and ethereal light about the place. Belém was founded in 1616, about the same time the Pilgrims were settling in the Massachusetts Bay area. The Spanish and Portuguese were battling for control of the area and the Portuguese won. They turned Belém into the major port of the Amazon.

Located on the banks of the Guamá River, one of the many tributaries that flow into the Amazon delta, about 100 miles from the Atlantic Ocean, Belém was situated on the river that was the major highway to the main body of the Amazon. It was an incredible distance from both Rio de Janeiro or São Paulo: legend has it, and I believe it, that the wealthy families in Belém up to the Republican period in 1889 used to send their laundry to Lisbon for washing because it was closer than Rio de Janeiro.

Here was a town with all the streets laid out with tremendous mango trees; their shade cover protected you from the brutal equatorial sun. The Portuguese had brought them from India and you would walk down a street in deep shade and never notice the burning sun. Mangos would fall from the trees when ripe but rumor had it they only hit tourists. The equal day and night of the equator fascinated me. There was no twilight there; one would walk down a street in the bright sunshine during the evening, and when you reached the end of the block it was pitch black.

Belém was very livable. You got up with the chickens and went to bed by 9 or 10 pm. We were a degree or so below the equator and you knew it; the heat slowly built up during the morning hours and by noon everyone was off the streets and having a two-hour lunch break. In the afternoon there would be a tremendous downpour, so constant you could set your watch by it. We made appointments to meet before the rain or after the rain. The heat and humidity would be stifling until the rain came, pouring down heavily for about twenty minutes, and then spring was in the air. Through the late afternoon it slowly heated up again and by the time sunset came the night air crept in. Evenings were amazing chilly; It was cool enough to sleep under a thin cotton blanket in a hammock if you felt the desire to do so. (My attempts to sleep in a hammock were disastrous. You had to sleep on your back.)

A Trip to the Beach

Life in Belém was always exciting, but at the time I did not know how exciting it would get. One Sunday, at a picnic on the island of Mosqueiro, I met and fell in love with a beautiful Brazilian girl named Dionir de Souza Gomes. This has been quite a romance, lasting 62 years.

But let's start at the beginning of this saga. There was a picnic on Mosqueiro, an island about twenty minutes from the city of Belém. The townspeople went there for a Sunday outing, and other families had summer houses there. It was on the sparkling Sunday morning of May 16, 1943 that Paul Oechsli and I decided to head for the island. We were off to see what luck we would have with the locals. Little did I know that destiny was riding on our next moves. There were a group of girls on the beach and we approached them stuttering and stammering in Portuguese. By this time we had been in Brazil long enough to speak Portuguese perfectly well (or at least we thought so).

We started with usual banter and soon we were into serious English teaching. I would draw a circle in the sand and say the word "moon" and the girls would chorus back "moon.' They would then say the word in Portuguese, "*lua,*" and Paul and I feeling like the village idiots would say the word "*lua*" back. This went on for hours and soon in the late afternoon we began to prepare for the return trip to Belém. One of the girls I fancied the most, a short, cute brunette, turned to the others and in Portuguese (that I was not meant to understand) said, "Hands off the short one with blue eyes. He is mine."

The future Mrs. Young had spoken. I opened my eyes as wide as they would go without falling out of their sockets.

On the way home I had the chance to ride in the Rubber Development Corporation boat and I asked a few of the girls if they wanted a ride. Dionir accepted and we draped ourselves over the railing to watch the Amazon go by. I talked to her in botched Portuguese while Dionir worked hard as she struggled with the English grammar and syntax. Then the unexpected happened: a man perched at the railing fell into the river and appeared to be drowning. I forgot that I was not supposed to speak Portuguese and began shouting orders to the pilot. "Throw out the life preserver!" - "Put the ship in neutral!" and Dionir kept urging me on. Suddenly she stopped and turned to me, her eyes blazing, and said, "I thought you didn't speak Portuguese." I explained that I knew a few words more than I'd admitted. She later told me that she decided right then and there to either murder me or marry me.

A very serious young man in his first white linen suit, and a tropical beauty named Dionir. Belém do Pará, 1943.

May 25, 1943

A nice wet, warm drizzly evening. I had thought that I had neglected this diary for the complete time I had been in Belém - so many things have happened since I arrived last Monday. I have been here over a week and it feels like a day. I have been working out at Tapaná constantly helping Lt. Rickheimer do the organizing of the camp. I got riled at first when he showed up but what the hell here is a guy with 35 years a partner in an engineering firm and has a home and wife etc. and is now doing the same thing that I am doing – so why get excited – just keep your mouth shut and your eyes open.

Well Saturday night I went to the casino which was horrible the less said about it the better. Sunday Paul (oh yes Paul is here) and I went to Mosqueiro on the steam boat. It took about 2 hours and two mil réis and we had to stand up all the time. There it seemed to Paul like Catalina Island.

The trip on the boat reminded me somewhat of the Rio Doce as the water is muddy as hell. At Mosqueiro we took a bus to Farol (lighthouse) and there rented a room for the day. Well there I met a girl named Dionir Gomes. If all Brazilian girls were like her I see little difficulty in an American falling in love with a Brazilian. She works in the Panair field and does work that we admire of girls back home. She is a dispatcher of airplanes. I don't know why but I am afraid that I like her very much. She made a wonderful day at Mosqueiro. We went back in the Rubber Reserve Boat and saved two men whose boat had overturned. The biggest problem was getting the nude man on the boat with all the girls watching.

Tired and weary but happy as all hell. I held hands with Dionir until the boat landed in Belém. I sure didn't need any inducement for sleep that night.

Monday we worked out a plan for the camp. And in the afternoon I talked with Piava and he had quite a cute secretary. Nothing very special that day- went to sleep at 9 o'clock. This morning I spent the morning and afternoon in the camp. Arriving in the evening back in Belém, we met Dionir and her sister who I don't like as much as her. Blonde etc. Made a date with the sec of our office tonight but game called on account of rain. Have date with Dionir for tomorrow to see the "cidade velho," the old city. Have my fingers crossed but funny I still do not know if I like Belém or not. I want to go back to Fortaleza. I miss Marinha and having her around amounted to more than I realized. I must write her a letter. Well I must write a report. The sight of those U.S. Planes over Val de Cães [airport] was a pretty sight. Also the use of a PX is wonderful.

May 26, 1943

I forgot Sunday a good piece of folklore. When we went swimming Dionir stopped before going in and drew a line around the outline of her foot and then put a cross in it and said we would not get bit.

Yesterday I was out at the camp until 3 o'clock in the afternoon. Then went to see Dionir and she showed me around the old city, a very beautiful cathedral, and some old cobblestone streets like old Portugal. Then at night we went to the movies and almost arrived late.

May 28, 1943

Gosh am I tired. Here I have been going out with Dionir and don't know if I like her or not. Funny smooching here in Brazil. It is difficult but it can be done – get to work, you have reports. Saturday afternoon in the office very still and very bad. Phooey. I wish I was on the beach comber in Fortaleza. Time has been zipping by so fast that I can't keep track of it.

At a beach house in Chapéu Virado, Mosqueiro. Dionir and I are the two on the far right.

I was supposed to leave this morning for Fortaleza but no plane so what the hell. The time I spent here zipped by what with work – Dionir - and a myriad of little things to do. I have not even had time to see the famous Indian museum but the most illuminating "signs of the times" comes when Dionir and I could not get into the museum because we were not properly chaperoned.

This place here is now crawling with English and RAF men.

We went to Mosqueiro with the Panair girls and wow! Down on the island Dionir really made me homesick or something. I have not figured it out. It is odd to make love in Portuguese especially those little meaningless words. I am glad to be going back to Fortaleza. I need a rest and it certainly can not be gotten here.

Return to Fortaleza

I stayed in Belém about three weeks before I returned to Fortaleza. Life in Fortaleza seemed dull and flat. Here are some letters to my parents:

June 8th 1943, Fortaleza, Ceará

Belém is already a bit different from Natal and Fortaleza. With 250,000 people, it is a tough job to keep tabs on people when they keep coming in and going out of the place so fast that it leaves even blasé Americans slightly bewildered.

But this is bringing me up to a point. I went and got myself a girl in Belém. I made sure that dating her a few times would not end up with poppa looming up behind me one night with a shotgun and muttering in Portuguese that this American would have to marry his daughter. Nothing but I do like her very much and the time I was in Belém we did see each other constantly. I broke a lot of taboos by seeing her as much as I did.

Being away from her and Belém for a week her letters were nice and regular. Oh yes, next month I may get transferred to Belém to work out of the office there. Our organization, if you can call it such, has been reorganized, and our boss here is now head of the new migration project. His name is Dr. Charles Wagley. I believe I have written about him before. He was switched to the central office in Rio de Janeiro to assist the Director of the Brazil field party. Dr. Wagley is a remarkable man. He was a professor of Anthropology at Columbia University and a graduate sociology student. He has made a study of an Indian tribe here in Brazil. They are called the Tapirapé Indians, and he lived with them for more than three months. He also married a Brazilian girl.

Oh yes I sold the horse which was a real nag and not fit for anything but the glue factory.

June 14th 1943, Fortaleza, Ceara

Well to say the least it was good to hear from Dad again. Wish you would make a point to stick in a few scribbled words in each letter because though they mean very little to you when you write them once they get down here – they are mighty important in the morale department. Glad to hear that you are working in your line again but as usual I would like some details if it is not war work. I mean who are you working for; what are you making a month; how much do I have to go to equal you; or I won't get there for the next 20 years.

Then the unbelievable news arrived that I had been transferred to the Amazon project - back to Belém.

Chapter 8. The Amazon Project (1943-44)

The move from Fortaleza to Belém was an exciting one - I was to be sent to the Amazon Project. Amid tearful farewells at the Fortaleza airport and promises to write everyone, I climbed into a C-47 U.S. Air Force plane and settled down on the metal seats that lined its side. No amenities here. About an hour and a half later we bounced into the Val de Cães airport in Belém do Pará at the mouth of the Amazon. The turbulence was wild but at the equator that was to be expected.

The Amazon Project

My job in the Amazon was coordinating all the reports that doctors would send in from the various outposts that they would visit. The size of the area just about boggled your mind. It was bigger than all of Europe and I was supposed to handle all the reporting from the area. Though this may have served the interests of the United Sates government - after all, we did want to get rubber out from the area - the health problems we tackled were ten times bigger than any rubber that we managed to gather.

Some history of the SESP (Serviço Especial de Saude Pública, or Special Service for Public Health) in the Amazon area would have to start with a Brazilian scientist, Oswaldo Cruz (1872-1917), who surveyed the Amazon Valley and suggested how the work was to be carried out. His report was made to Sergio Castro during World War I. The report lay dormant until Getúlio Vargas visited the area in 1941 and outlined his "March to the West." Brazil's destiny, Vargas proclaimed, was to be found in expanding west up

Paul Oechsli (right) and Jordan in front of a typical SESP hospital on the Amazon.

the Amazon. The first Cruz report was carried forward by Carlos Chagas, whose untimely death in 1934 prevented him from seeing the final study and implementation as it developed under the SESP, but by that time Brazilian political leaders had firmly placed the Amazon on the political map of the country. The SESP was set up during World War II by agreements between the Brazilian and American governments in 1942. It was one branch of the Institute of Inter-American Affairs, where Nelson Rockefeller had the title of Coordinator of Inter-American Affairs.

An example of how we operated was the case of Dr. Albino Figueiredo, who was stationed in the subdistrict of Chaves, about 100 miles from Belém. He sought to construct a medical outpost in which to improve the living conditions of our doctors, study the water supply and sewage conditions, and hype our educational program. Among the diseases treated were malaria, worms, dysentery, pneumonia, and Chagas disease. Chagas disease was caused by a bug that crawled out from the mud walls at night while you were sleeping and, after biting you, laid some eggs in your bloodstream and then lived the rest of its life multiplying with you as the host family.

Dr. Einor Hugo Christopherson[44], Chief of the Field Party in Brazil, called me in one day. He issued a travel authorization dated December 31, 1943, stipulating that I could travel to all points within the Amazon Project. I was authorized to travel if necessary by special authority, which meant by any means possible. My title would be officially that of Sociologist. I was one happy camper. Once I had to rent a mule when I travelled up to Santarém, a major town between Belém and Manaus. The controller's office asked me for a receipt for that episode, but found the mule story so unbelievable that I had to make one up.

A Delicate Mission

A few months into my stay in the Amazon project, Dr. Christopherson again called me into his office and said, "I have delicate mission for you. There is a United States Army mapping crew here and they want to borrow one of our SESP boats for a mapping project up the Amazon. We know they'll swipe the boat if they get a chance and take it all the way to Peru and then junk it. We value the few boats we have. Can you keep an eye on them and stop them from stealing the boat?" That started me on the most bizarre escapade of my Amazon adventures.

Planning for the trip began immediately. We loaded supplies on the SESP boat at night, as we were to leave at the crack of dawn to catch the tides and currents as we crossed the delta to the main stream of the Amazon. The launch resembled the African Queen of Bogart and Hepburn: three bunks and a small galley. The pilot was also our cook. We made it through the Straits of Breves and by dawn we were well into the main stream of the Amazon.

The job of the army team, as I understood it, was to map the main course of the Amazon. We would stop in the evening, wait until midnight, and take an azimuth reading. This was accomplished by getting the BBC on the short wave radio at midnight and then recording where we were. It was an eerie feeling as we tuned into the BBC a few minutes before midnight and heard the music hall comediennes telling jokes. We would laugh and heard laughter from

---

[44] According to Dr. Christopherson's obituary in the *Deseret News* of August 22, 1997, "During World War II his task, as chief of a Brazilian field party, Office of International Affairs, was to keep laborers physically fit and working to produce critical products. The success of this program, involving thousands of workers and a staff of 300 doctors, nurses, and technicians, brought him a citation from the Brazilian government."

Jordan and the Pará, our SESP vessel.

all around the circle beyond our camp. There was always a circle of invisible guests, local villagers and Indians who lived out in the forest. Then the bong, bong, bong of Big Ben and the clipped words of the announcers, "This is 12 midnight Greenwich mean time."

Often we would stop at various trading posts along the way. We would see the rubber workers (*seringueiros*) lined up waiting to get paid for the rubber they had brought in. The company stores generally ripped off the rubber workers. The storekeeper would give the rubber worker credit for rubber they would bring in on their next trip and let them run up a generous tab. Unfortunately the amount of rubber brought in was never equal to the amount of credit given, and the charges were never paid off. Prices for store bought goods were terribly inflated. A worker kept owing the store owner money and that debt would be carried on by their children. It was a death sentence to try and run away from your debts: the store owner always had *capangas*, or hired gunmen, who would hunt you or your children down.

Many years later Warren Dean wrote that the typical seringueiro was paid three cruzeiros, or roughly 15 cents, per kilogram, while the storekeeper that sold him his supplies received an additional 1.25 cruzeiros. As people lined up for the payments, we took advantage of the fact and gave them atebrine (mepacrine) pills. It may have made them piss bright yellow but it helped with malaria. To encourage the seringueiros to take the pills, we told them it made them more virile.

The way the seringueiros prepared the rubber biscuits allowed for a little deceit on the part of the rubber gatherers. The liquid latex they took from the trees looked like sticky cow's milk and would be poured over a paddle and held over a smoky flame until it hardened into a "biscuit." While this process was going on a few rocks would be added to the latex to increase the weight. Of course the purchasers suspected this and every once in a while they would slice a biscuit in half and see if any stones were embedded in it.

One night at twilight we anchored in an *igarape* (a small inlet off the Amazon) and suddenly we heard screams way off in the distance, blood-curdling yells that sounded just like human voices. I remember grabbing my rifle and reminding myself that this was the 20th century and that things like this did not happen, that everything had a scientific explanation. The screams kept getting closer to the boat. I gripped the rifle tighter and had goose pimples waiting to see what would happen. Soon the screaming mass hit us and just as quickly subsided as a huge collection of monkeys sailed over our boat and us and continued on their way.

Seringueiros lined up for payday.

We ate at the boarding houses up the Amazon. The food was simple but adequate. Eating my beans and rice one night I noticed a boa constrictor curled up in a dark corner. I edged out of my chair and went to the owner of the *pensão*. He checked it out and assured me that boas were a common sight in the boarding houses - they were kept as house pets because they were able to control the rat population. He calmed me down and said that he could always get paying guests, but a good boa was hard to find.

That night, as I checked the mosquito net over my hammock, I thought I heard the sharp nails of a rat on the tile roof of the house. The sound was followed by the slither of the boa and then a crunch as he enveloped the rat, though this may have been my imagination. I did not sleep well that night.

Once we pulled into a collection of huts that passed for a town and traded our C-rations for fresh chickens. Then we arrived at the Jari River, which comes down from the Guyana frontier, where all the gold and diamond smuggling in the region went on. We went up the Jari as far as the falls and then anchored our boat. There we were invited to visit the local land baron and his plantation, which was similar to any Indian trading post on the Amazon.

Typical rubber biscuit production, 1944.

Abandoned mansion on the Xingu, likely that of a rubber baron from the 1890's Rubber Boom.

The "baron" (*barão*) had heard a story that the Americans were interested in buying his plantation and turning it into a huge international airport. This sort of rumor made you wonder about the perennial fears that the Brazilians have about the Amazon, the "last bastion" of natural wealth for the nation, being stolen from them or, in this case, making a fortune from the sale. We allowed that we were not the advance party for this project. The plantation owner was a throwback to colonial times. An obese man in a hammock, he was surrounded by young Indian and mulatto girls, who fanned him and hovered over him.

The vultures, which are the garbage collectors of the Amazon, come in surprising colors. Their plumage runs all colors of the rainbow. Much to my amazement, I shot one when I least expected it. I was in the bow of the boat and saw a vulture. I slowly raised my rifle and fired, and there was an explosion of feathers as the bird fell into river. I had provided a meal for some hungry crocodiles.

We reached the Tapajós River and the town of Santarém, about 600 miles from Belém. The blue water of the Tapajós flows into the brown of the Amazon and the two rivers do not mix for many miles. In Santarém there were instructions for me: I was to leave the boat and return to Belém. I never knew what happened to our boat. Many years later I was surprised to see Lt. Gilmor, one of the mapping crew on that expedition, behind the circulation desk of the University of California library.

Life in and Around Belém

Vendors' tents at the Cirio de Nazaré.

Paul and I found ourselves one day in Santarém. We were hunkered down in our work clothes near one of our unfinished hospitals, talking together in English. Several dollar-a-year men[45] came by and marveled at our English. They figured we were descendants from the old civil war colony and began to question us. "Where did you learn your English?" We said our parents had taught us. No lie there. "Do you want to go to the U.S.A.?" We said sure. And they went away muttering to themselves. We would have jumped into the river if he had offered us some coins to fetch.

Artur Cesar Fereira Reis[46], a professor of Brazilian history, was born in the city of Belém and an ardent booster of the town. He would take me on walking tours of the old city and fill me with the folklore of the area. One was that girls would walk at night along the river banks and come home pregnant, claiming that the *boto* (a fresh water dolphin) had made them pregnant.

We would stand before those old colonial churches and ponder the wonderful baroque lines. Professor Reis pointed out that often it was Indian labor that went into those elaborate designs. One

---

45 Business and government executives from the United States who volunteered to help with the war effort and were paid a token salary by the U.S. Government.

46 During the military dictatorship he became military governor of the state of Amazonas.

particularly famous church was *Nossa Senhora de Nazaré*, where the people of Belém celebrated a festival called the *Cirio de Nazaré.* Thousands of people came from the interior and turned the square into a huge open air bazaar. The food that appeared on the stands produced the most tantalizing aromas: there was mouth-watering *manicoba*, which was made from the ground up leaves of *manieva* plant and a variety of smoked meats; turtles of all sizes and descriptions, and delicious crab meat covered with toasted manioc flour.

Nearby was the Museu Goeldi, which Dionir and I would visit on Sundays. We could go chaperoned or unchaperoned and catch a few torrid necking scenes amid the wildlife. We also took a weird trip to the town of Cametá, upstream from Belém, about which I remember only that we tied up our boat at the foot of the street and walked up to the still, shadowy town.

Often we would travel on the PBYs, flying boats that were used up and down the river. It was a weird sensation to sit in the plane as it taxied for a take-off and see the water rushing by your window. The greatest fear that pilots had was that some log-like shape would turn out to not be a crocodile and would rip a hole in the plane as it roared down the river

The Japanese Colony

On August 13, we left Belém aboard the SESP launch Pará bound for the Acará River. The purpose of our trip was to visit Tomé-Açu, an area settled by Japanese. Most of them had arrived in 1929 and turned the area into a thriving supplier of fresh vegetables and hot peppers for Belém. At the behest of the American government, the Brazilians had taken the thriving agricultural area that the Japanese had cultivated and declared it an internment camp. We were going to inspect the many health outposts that SESP had set up to protect the health of rubber workers in the region. The expedition was to leave a little before midnight so that we could catch the tides, which would place us in the main stream of the Amazon by morning, well on our way to Tomé-Açu.

We went up the Moju River to get to the Acará River where the Japanese colony was located. Dr. Robert Payne was the MD in charge of the expedition and told how he was forced out of Bolivia because of a run-in with the American ambassador there (I never asked about the details). At one point someone shouted "*jacaré*" (a reptile similar to a crocodile or alligator), and I grabbed my rifle hoping to bag one. You had to shoot a *jacaré* right between the eyes or else it did nothing, and the animal would simply slip away. These things took bullets all over their bodies and nothing but a shot between the eyes could kill them. There were also the reliable *urubu*, (vultures), which I hated with a deep revulsion. They stank as they tore up the entrails of the animal they were eating.

We stopped at a trading post called Moderne and bought a chicken, sugar, and some bananas. We tied up at the dock of some "*commerciante*" at about 5 in the afternoon and it was raining cats and dogs; there seems to be nothing wetter than a rainstorm in the Amazon River. People gave us everything we wanted, including one drink that was called the *Caboclo Innocente* ("the Innocent Hick" in English), a powerful local corn liquor.

As we got closer to Tomé-Açu, I became a little bit apprehensive about the situation. Yes, we knew that the place had been turned into a Japanese internment camp. There were approximately 2,000 people living in the camp, people who emigrated from Japan many years prior to the war seeking a new life in the Amazon. We heard that the colony had declined to about 700 Japanese families, plus a few Germans and other "enemy aliens" living there.

Dr. Payne, the leader of our group of four, assured us that there was nothing to worry about as the men at Tomé-Açu were just farmers. I was nervous because the Japanese seemed to have an

Young Japanese men at the docks.

inordinate number of rifles and I thought they might use them on us. The Japanese were probably more scared of us than we of them, and handled us with kid gloves. Tomé-Açu had been designated as a internment camp, but all this really meant was that the Brazilian authorities had taken down the sign that indicated that the Japanese agricultural colony existed and replaced it with another. There was no indication of a military presence.

We arrived at about noon and were greeted by a Brazilian who escorted us to the hospital. They had the best hospital around; we saw medical supplies there that vastly surpassed anything we provided for our simple medical outposts. We saw posters in Japanese about eye diseases and malaria. Some of them had English translations underneath, but no Portuguese. Everyone was friendly and cheerful.

One of the Germans interred at Tomé-Açu, in charge of the local hospital, was an exchange professor of zoology. He'd been completing his Ph.D. thesis when the war broke out. He looked like an advertisement for the perfect German - six feet tall, blond hair, blue eyes, and immaculately dressed. He wouldn't let me take his picture. Maybe he was a spy and a Nazi, but what he would spy about in Tomé-Açu I will never know.

I felt funny walking through the camp, meeting groups of Germans and Japanese who spoke halting English. I got to talking with one Japanese man and when I asked what he did for recreation, I was baffled by the reply as he asked me if I could send him some baseballs. We left the camp feeling there was no threat to national security, and having tasted the best food in the valley. We loaded up with fresh fruits and vegetables before we left.

We arrived back in Belém after 11 pm on August 17 and there was no car to meet us so Dr. Payne and I took the streetcar home. It was a fitting end to high adventure.

Another Trip

These trips were like drugs to me. On August 22, we were off again. We now headed for Cametá, a former capital of the state of Pará, on the River Tocantins. There I met an Indian agent, a government official from the *Serviço de Proteção ao Índio* (Indian Protection Service, or SPI) in charge of contact with the indigenous people. The agent was vivid in his description of his meeting with

One of the Japanese inhabitants of Tomé-Açu. Despite the great number of rifles present they were very hospitable.

the Indians and was disgruntled with the order from Rio that they could not carry a gun. He claimed that Indians were chasing settlers into the towns, arriving spread out, so he would have to figure out who was the chief. The agent had been with General Cândido Mariano da Silva Rondon, a pioneer in the support of Brazilian Indians. He always wore a metal bulletproof vest, even through he would always be unarmed. God, it must have been sweltering to wear body armor in a climate like that.

Last Notes on Belém

The dating game in Belém, as practiced in the 1930s and 1940s, was an elaborate courting routine that was called "footing." You could not properly speak to a young lady unless you'd been properly introduced to her. To accomplish this purpose all the young men would walk around the square and all the young women would walk in counter clockwise fashion so that you would pass all the girls. Does it sound absurd or not? I couldn't date Dionir without a chaperone. We'd go to the movies accompanied by one, the three of us walking into the theater together. Once inside, everyone would change seats when the lights dimmed so you could be alone.

I never saw the end of any movie in the time I was in Belém, as I was busy returning to my seat.

About this time I had a strange meeting with an FBI man. There was no CIA then and the job of ferreting out Communists and watching the enemy fell to the FBI. You could always spot those guys because they spoke perfect Spanish and had trench coats that were all alike. I wondered whether they'd been issued from a central warehouse in Washington.

I was drinking at a local bar and someone introduced me to the local FBI agent. Meeting a fellow American was all that was necessary to start a conversation in those days. We got to talking about many things, and as sex was always on my mind in one form or another we finally came to said topic. I'd had sex two years ago in São Paulo and simply told him that I was feeling raunchy. He admitted to knowing a discrete house behind the Grand Hotel, and he said that if I went there at two in the afternoon I would be "taken care of." Two in the afternoon in Belém do Pará is probably the one time that chances of meeting anyone you know, let alone seeing someone out on the streets, were remote. No one went out in that blazing hot sun.

Thus, at two in the afternoon, I timidly knocked on the discrete house's door and a servant girl let me in. What would happen next? I was escorted into a small room and there was young girl, fashionably dressed in white. She smiled hello. I gulped. What do I do now? She apparently knew the ropes and quickly undressed me and then nature took its course. I remember that I left money, which she counted carefully and in turn left some to the lady who owned the house and left. Memories are tricky things and it was not great sex, certainly not like the São Paulo encounter.

That should be the end of that story but it wasn't. The society of Belém had tea dances on Sundays. I went to one because I knew that many of Belém's most eligible women would be there, and it was the "in" thing to do. Lo and behold, there was the young lady in white with whom I had spent time with only a week before, dancing primly with her partner. I was embarrassed and tried to hide my face and asked discretely who she was. She was identified as the daughter of the state of Pará's Secretary of Agriculture.

Missing Home

When I was deep up the river I would dream of what foods I missed most of all. The item that continually flashed before my mind was a Nedick's frankfurter, an orange soda, and a thick chocolate milkshake. In these bouts of nostalgia I would crack open bottles of *guaraná*, a local soft drink that tasted like vanilla cream soda.

Dionir and I had a falling out. This was for the better, as we were both too young to make a serious commitment. (I was 23 and she was 21.) She asked Panair do Brasil for a job transfer to Rio de Janeiro and I decided to get serious about getting back to the U.S.A. Her job in Rio was an interesting one: she worked as a stewardess on the short flight from Rio to São Paulo. She'd been at this for six months when a fellow worker asked Dionir to swap shifts with her because of a medical appointment. Di happily obliged. However, the plane that Dionir would have been on crashed, killing her friend, and Dionir's picture appeared in the papers as one of the missing crew members. Her parents made her quit soon after that.

By this time it was 1944 and I really wanted to go home and join the Army. I felt the war was passing me by and I had contributed all that I wanted to contribute to Brazil. I began preparations for the flight to the U.S.A.

Chapter 9.
The Army (1944-45)

I wanted to engage in combat with either Germans or Japanese. It made no difference to me: the American mindset at the time was that both were evil and we were the good guys. I wanted to get into the Army and to do that I would have to get a ride on an U.S. Air Force plane headed for Miami from Belém. After much talking and headshaking the Chief Operations Officer allowed me to grab a seat on a plane and I was off. One small suitcase with some samba records and dressed in my best white linen suit and I was there. I was sitting in those tin buckets that served as seats in a C-47 transport plane bound for the U.S.A.

Eight hours later the neon signs and twinkling lights of Miami could be seen from the porthole of the plane and we swooped into the airport. I got off and heaved a great sigh of relief when a Military Policeman approached me and asked to see my draft card and passport. He glanced oddly at my white suit while I cheerfully told him I had no draft card and had arrived in the U.S.A. to join the army. He looked puzzled and asked if I was 18, to which I said no, I was 23.

"Well, where the hell have you been for the last four years?" he asked. "Working up the Amazon River," I replied, to which he said, "A likely story. I'm afraid you'll have to be detained while we check that out." He took my passport, which established that I was an American citizen and was employed by the U.S. Government in the Amazon.

So I arrived at the Battle Creek Hotel in Miami under house arrest and placed in protective custody. Thus began my saga to get into the U.S. Army. Incredible as it may sound some official in Brazil managed to contact some bureaucrat in the U.S.A. within the week, and I was free to proceed to New York. But my problems were just beginning.

After a crowded train trip to the Big City - where I wanted to tell a bored bunch of New Yorkers about my Amazon adventures - I arrived home. I finally had the Nedick's frank that I had promised myself in Brazil.

I went to the draft registration office in Washington Heights where my folks had been living. We used to have a nice apartment across the street from Colombia Presbyterian Hospital, but they moved to Flushing in the borough of Queens. With butterflies in my throat, I went into the Selective Service office where I used to live. A little old lady in white sneakers greeted me warmly and I gave her my name and said I would like to join the army. She walked over to her files. After a few moments she turned and beamed a bright smile at me saying, "If you are Jordan Young, you're supposed to be working up the Amazon River." I patiently explained that I was now in the U.S.A. and wanted to join the army and needed a draft card to establish my identity. She seemed slightly miffed and informed me that she kept the best records of any Selective Service Board in the U.S.A., and her records indicated I was in Brazil. I repeated that I was in the U.S.A. now and could I please have my draft card. She answered that until she heard from Brazil I was in Brazil as far she was concerned, and that was that. "Don't worry," she said, "when I hear anything I'll let you know."

So began a saga that every time I passed a Military Policeman I cringed and my stomach muscles tensed up for fear I would hear the magic words, "Can I please see your draft card?"

I tried to enlist in Washington, D.C. and I almost succeeded. When the interview was over, the recruiter casually asked me if I had a draft classification. "Nope" I answered, "just that I'm registered at some Selective Service Board in Manhattan and they can't process my name because —" He never let me finish and said, "I'm sorry. I can't touch you because I'll be accused of stealing men from your local draft board."

Crestfallen, I returned to New York doomed like a man without a country. I could not be drafted, I could not enlist. I was sure I would be discovered and shot as a deserter.

The War Department Translation Branch

Life travels in funny circles. In February 1944 I was standing on the corner of 6th Ave and 42nd Street waiting for a bus. Across the street was a store with the words United States Information Service[47] blazoned across the front. I stuck my nose in and asked whether they might have some use for a person who spoke Portuguese. The sergeant in charge said there was an installation that worked with foreign languages at 165 Broadway - the Chemical Bank building - and if I went to the 17th floor I might check it out.

The office number I had written down was 1701 and I rapped on the door. The door was cautiously opened by a civilian and I explained that I had just returned from Brazil and spoke fluent Portuguese. He told me to wait a minute and called someone. The next man asked me to pronounce the capital of Brazil, followed by "good morning" and "how are you" in Portuguese. He seemed satisfied and informed me that this was not a draft deferred job which was okay with me. He explained that I had walked into the War Department's language unit[48] and I could have the job of Portuguese language specialist. I grabbed it and for the next four months I was surrounded by an astounding group of men and women who were the most distinguished linguists in the world.

My job consisted in writing sentences in Portuguese for those booklets they gave to soldiers when they went overseas. Where is the railroad station? Where is the local bar? Could you please direct me to a restaurant? Where is the bathroom?

In addition there were foreign nationals from the four corners of the globe. Tagalog, Mandarin Chinese, German, and Russian were among the many languages spoken there. We would test out words to see if their English comprehension was deep enough. For example take the word "deck." Get me a deck of cards; go below the deck; she is all decked out; hit the deck - words that could be baffling unless you were a native speaker of English.

On dull days limericks were the order of day and we pumped out such magnificent examples as

[47] Originally the Allied Information Service (AIS) and later renamed the U.S. Information Agency (USIA).

[48] It might have been the Translation Branch of the Military Intelligence Service of the U.S. War Department.

There once was a girl from Cape Cod
who thought babies came from God.
She thought the Almighty
had lifted her nightie
but it was Roger the Lodger by God.

This lasted until July 1944, when the inevitable letter informed me that my friends and neighbors had decided that I had to report for induction into the army.

The Sanitary Corps

The next chapter in my education began when I was being interviewed by a regular army sergeant in the Induction Center. The first question concerned what I had done in civilian life. I was at a loss but told him that I was a sociologist and worked up the Amazon River. "Damn it," he replied, "I don't care what political party you were in. I want to know what you did in civilian life."

"Okay," I said, and then went on to patiently explain what a sociologist did. Please keep in mind that I was a person with only three years of college education and one course in sociology taken in Brazil. "We took a reading of the people of the Amazon Valley and studied the way they were. This was of a political nature, their views on life, what they ate, and finally," I concluded, "we did sanitary studies of the region." He looked at me and said "Did you

Alas, I did not take the Army very seriously.

In full "battle dress" in front of the barracks at Fort Lewis.

say sanitary studies? You're now in the Sanitary Corps." Off I went with another pre-med student to Fort Lewis, Washington to join the 161st Medical Battalion for training. What a blast.

I never took the army seriously and they returned the compliment. If you had a college degree, you would be promoted to Sgt. or Lt. and put over us G.I.s. Without such a degree I was a grunt. I actually enjoyed the training and I was to be the seventh man in a seven-man combat team. Rumors were that we would be posted to the China Burma India (CBI) theater of war. I was issued a Red Cross patch but was told not to wear it in the CBI theater, because if I did I'd be the first man shot by the Japanese.

On April 12, 1945, I was in the barracks when a radio announced that FDR had died. I sat down on the bed and thought about what that meant and tried not to weep. He was, after all, the only president I had ever really known.

Being of curious mind, I read all the bulletin boards in the training camp. One of them said that medical corpsmen were eligible for an advanced training course at Washington & Lee University in Lexington, Virginia. The course was called Educational Reconditioning, which involved dealing with amputee victims. I decided to sign up.

Two weeks before my unit was to be shipped out to CBI, there arrived a notice that Private Young was to report for duty in

Lexington, Virginia for the special course in Educational Reconditioning. Lexington is a good 3,000 miles from Ft. Lewis but the orders were cut by the sergeant in charge. I packed up my duffel back and off I went by train, first class. I spent the month learning how to deal with trauma victims, amputees, and other soldiers who had been shot up in the war.

When it was over another soldier and I decided to hitchhike to Washington, D.C. and then catch a train to Tacoma, Washington. It was easy to catch rides in those days, and being in uniform made it all the easier. As luck would have it, a station wagon passed us, backed up, and we were picked up by two middle-aged women. They let us off in a small town and said we wouldn't have any trouble getting a ride from there to Washington, D.C. But it seemed our luck had run out, as we ended up sticking our thumbs out for an hour.

At that point, a small child came out from the house we were in front of and said, "You are wanted on the phone!" Baffled, we went in the house, figuring it must be some mistake. It was the ladies who had left us off about an hour ago. They wanted know if we would have dinner with them, spend the night at their home, and continue on to Washington the next day.

We thanked the family for the use of the phone. The station wagon showed up after twenty minutes and we piled in. Visions of a wild night with some sex-starved housewives evaporated as we

Pit stop at Welbourne, Middleburg, Virginia.

drove up to a huge estate with antlers above the main entrance. We were escorted to a wing of the house and told that drinks would be served as soon as we freshened up.

The rest of the story was a dream-like sequence in which we were treated to an elaborate dinner with black servants behind each chair. This was Welbourne, the Middleburg, Virginia residence of Mr. and Mrs. N. H. Morrison[49]. They asked us questions about our army training. We recounted our stories and they listened politely.

Madigan General Hospital

We got back to Fort Lewis, Washington in one piece and I went in search of my unit. Empty barracks indicated that the unit had shipped out to the China Burma India theater and there I was, high and dry without a unit. I was assigned to KP duty with every unit in Camp Murray.

I was hitchhiking between Camp Murray, where our training was taking place, and the main installations of Madigan General, when a beat-up car stopped and the driver apologized that front seat was so messy that I would have to sit in the back. I climbed into back seat amid a pile of books and magazines. One of them turned out to be an issue of *The New Republic* and I ventured the opinion that I felt kind of funny seeing a liberal publication so far from New York City. He answered, "We're not all yahoos out here," and introduced himself as Carlin Aden. Later I found out he was the Poet Laureate of the State of Washington and taught Spanish at Madigan General Hospital.

Aden told me that my talents were wasted in the medical corps and got me an appointment to Madigan General Hospital Corp as a language specialist and foreign language instructor. There I remained until the war was over, giving lectures to the soldiers and signing up enlisted men for college courses.

---

[49] Welbourne is now a bed and breakfast inn. It is owned by an eighth generation family and covers 520 acres in the Piedmont Hunt Country. The main house dates from 1770 with additions as late as 1870. The house is a Virginia Historic Landmark and is on the National Register of Historic Places. Visitors during the Civil War included Jeb Stuart and John S. Mosby. In the 1930's F. Scott Fitzgerald and Thomas Wolfe stayed at Welbourne, both of whom published stories using the house as the setting. The website does not list the fact that Jordan Young stayed there in 1944.

On the typewriter at Madigan general, 1945.

Three memories from this period stand out in my mind – one was living off-post at the Aden residence; the second was the party we threw for the two Brazilian Army colonels I met in Tacoma, Washington; and the third was the mysterious Lt. Marjorie Montague.

The Two Brazilian Colonels

My encounter with the two Brazilian colonels is the best story of the three. Saturday night in Tacoma was pure bedlam as soldiers poured in and out of bars or just wandered the streets. Private Young was one of those lost souls when walking along, I noticed two officers with the word Brazil written above their army patches.

I didn't think twice about dashing up to them and saluting. In perfect Brazilian Portuguese I said I had been in Brazil for nearly three years. Although I was a private and they were officers, they were happy to talk to me. One thing led to another and I invited them to visit Madigan General Hospital. Privates don't typically ask colonels to visit them, but military protocol was not something I understood too clearly.

It was agreed that we would meet in front of the hospital the next Wednesday. The two foreign officers arrived in a staff car and before I could say anything a military policeman yelled "Atten-hut! We have foreign brass visiting the hospital – call the commanding General." I tried to explain that it was an informal visit but the MP turned to me and said, "Get lost, private." Neither Brazilian colonel spoke English and after we got things straightened out I was busy interpreting.

There was a lengthy tour of the installations, during which one of the officers whispered to me in Portuguese, "*Onde estão as moças de Cruz Vermerlho?*" ("Where are the Red Cross girls?"). I got the message; I told the Colonel that there would be girls and a party Friday night, at our house off-post.

Come Friday, Col. Carlos de Albuquerque and Lt. Col. João de Abreu were inducted into the world of Private Jordan Young. All I remember of the party was that the Colonel was on the floor with two bottles in his mouth and some girl was trying to toss cherries in the middle to complete a perfect Manhattan[50].

Living Off Base

I was able to live off the army base because another soldier by the name of Robert Levine and I rented a small house on a pond of water that had the regal sounding name of Lake Louise. What I remember about Sgt. Levine (my future neighbor in Princeton and father of my son's wife) was that he made egg omelets on the stove in the living room, and used them to entice some awfully attractive Red Cross nurses and sundry members of the WAC Corp into the house. We used to keep score over the bed of how many we seduced. Little did we know that the women were also keeping score.

The army provided the necessary background for my education on sex, although we were warned by constant films alerting us to the dangers of syphilis and gonorrhea. But we plunged in with wartime dedication. I will spare you the details, but there were maps on the ceiling that would only be seen to their advantage lying in

[50] I ran into Gen. Albuquerque seven years later, when I was working with a Chase Bank affiliate in Brazil as an investment banker trainee in Rio. See Chapter 13.

bed. That was my idea since I always wanted to follow the war carefully.

Carlin Aden invited me to live with him off-post, so I told Sgt. Levine to bag it, I'd had enough of omelets, and I was going to live with a family. We parted ways and I ended up on the second floor of the Aden residence.

I had not been living there more than a month in this charming Cape Cod when their niece Franny Crisswell showed up. Franny resembled one of those girls from the Lil Abner cartoon, buxom, seventeen years old, and known (to me, anyway) as Baby. The Adens pulled me aside and told me that she was a virgin and that they would like her to remain that way if I wanted to stay with them. I said okay - as long as we had to live under the same roof, I was a gentleman. We had adjoining rooms on the second floor. She pursued me relentlessly. On moonlit nights she'd come into my room, lie down on my bed, and ask me to tell her stories about Brazil. I was true to the letter of my word – we did everything but have intercourse. I claim that I got asthma as result of getting too little sleep.

One day she came into my room and told me that she'd had sex with a lieutenant so she was no longer a virgin. But I'd made a promise, and the Adens wouldn't have known about her change in status.

Picnic at Fort Lewis, Carlin Aden in the back wearing a white shirt, and Franny Crisswell to his right.

Lt. Marjorie Montague

The story of Lt. Marjorie Montague is much more complicated, but perhaps I have made it more complicated than it actually is. She was an officer in the physiotherapy corps of the hospital, and I was a private. The two do not mix well.

One day something was wrong with my back and I went down to the physiotherapy department for treatment. Lt. Montague and I got to talking, and she seemed intrigued that I that I had been in Brazil. One thing led to another and we became fast friends. She was blond with blue eyes but she was a dry woman, nothing cordial about her.

She led me into mountain climbing and we explored the terrain around the fort, including the small towns that dot the Puget Sound area. We were more like two people who had the same interests rather than a love affair. The difficulty was the she was a lieutenant and I was a private. It did not seem to faze either of us a bit. She

Lt. Montague and I on a hiking excursion, 1945.

seemed dedicated to causes and often tried to get me to join organizations of one kind or another. But most of all I enjoyed the physiotherapy sessions a great deal.

The War Ends

Peace came with I was still at Madigan General Hospital, on August 14, 1945. The negotiations had been going on for days - would they surrender?

August 10, 1945

God, what a tremendous earth-shaking event has been taking place today. I can simply say that Japan has surrendered and not yesterday's announcement of Russia's declaration of war against Japan or the atomic bomb or M.M.'s leaving. Atom bombs! War! Peace!

August 11, 1945

News of the world still bouncing like a ping-pong ball. Since Wednesday it has been one earth-shaking event after another. Earth is right - the atomic bomb dropped on the city of Hiroshima (odd how familiar with the names in Japan become). The Japs have offered to surrender but want to keep their Emperor in power. They just got the Allied counter proposal.

August 14, 1945, 4 p.m.

It's here - Japan has surrendered officially. I didn't want to be in an office in a hospital when the war ended. Yet it was unavoidable - I guess - when returning the the U.S.A. I felt that I could make my choice but it just happened. Just after Steffler and I were sitting in the office, he remarked that he couldn't feel happy thinking of all the men who had died.

I feel the job of the war is just beginning. The radio is blaring from Times Square. It is moving - a mass emotional jag.

How did I feel about the atomic bomb? Nothing about the horror of it: the only question was, Would it end the war today, or tomorrow? When they dropped the second bomb, I just said "Okay, maybe we'll need a third." We all wanted the war to end and the sooner the better. There was no morality involved. The Japanese had been killing Americans and the Americans were killing Japanese and with the atomic bomb that was over, period. My chances of living through the whole thing had increased considerably. I got a three-day pass and went out to celebrate.

Only later did I being to have doubts about the decision. The number of casualties that they expected were inflated and the Japanese were trying to surrender via the Russians when we sent off the second atomic bomb. Much later on I rethought the whole thing again after reading the book *Downfall* by Richard Frank, which claims that the Japanese would never have surrendered.

We were demobilized in July, 1946. I hitchhiked from California home to New York which was particularly easy for a serviceman at the time. I had to make up my mind what university to go to. The universities were all appealing to the G.I.'s. The University of Chicago urged me to join them but the flat streets of Chicago could not compete with the University of California at Berkeley, with San Francisco across the bay. Chicago reminded me too much of the crazier aspects of Rio de Janeiro and made it easy for me to say no. I decided to go to Berkeley.

Chapter 10. Back to the University: U.C. Berkeley (1945-46)

I had a love affair with the University of California and San Francisco. When I visited San Francisco it was if I were taking a trip back to Rio de Janeiro. I took to it like a duck to water. These two years of my life were the happiest I can remember before getting married.

The year was 1946 and the utter confusion at the university was complete. Returning soldiers flooded the campus by the thousands. The registrar was most cooperative and willing to grant me credit for the courses I had taken before from the University of Illinois and - much to my amazement - the courses I had taken at the Brazilian universities. This left me with upper junior status and less than a year and half to go for my degree.

UC Berkeley had a quaint custom of demanding that entering students state their religious preference. I decided that Zoroastrian would be an adequate answer; it just seemed wild and far out. The university officials never bothered me about it. But I did not count on the Zoroastrian Society sending me a note asking that I attend their next meeting.

Classes at Berkeley

The arrogance of the returning GI's was something to see. Professors were challenged by students as never before. One had to be in the situations to believe them. In some classes battle-hardened veterans were listening to some young graduate student sound off. In others, professors simply didn't knowing their material or it was out of date. I had one such case: the professor - supposedly a specialist on Latin America - was going on about Brazil and I could not take any more of it and challenged some of the things he said. I learned my lesson when I received the only B I got in my courses at Berkeley.

It was a weird sensation when I went from a straight C at the University of Illinois to a straight A student at Berkeley. It is amazing what a few years can do to one's perspective and motivation.

A few of us would get together after class and discuss the material and then at exam time write up questions that we thought the professor would ask. We hit the head on the nail so many times that the professor thought we had the questions beforehand or were cheating.

Classes were so large that some bright student invented Phi Beta notes[51] in which he took the professor's notes down from the previous semester, had them mimeographed, and sold them to eager incoming students. As we listened to the professor all you could hear was the rustling of pages as students followed along in the notes. One day one of the professors departed from his notes and I heard an angry voice from among the students saying, "The son of a bitch is ad-libbing."

One teacher stood out in my mind - Prof. Engel Sluiter. His passionate interest was the Dutch period in Brazil, 1630-1645. Anything that could be known about Brazil in the 1630s he knew. He never published much and it was always said that when he died, some graduate student would inherit his notes and make a reputation with them. His seminars in the evening were ulcer-makers. They were so stressful that I sometimes wouldn't eat dinner for fear that it would come back during his seminar.

It was at Berkeley that I learned that I was as smart as anybody and when it came to Latin American, I was smarter. That was most amazing to me.

I don't know how I found the *Daily Californian*, the newspaper of UC Berkeley[52]. The *Daily Cal* was loaded with a talented and

---

[51] Named after the Phi Beta Kappa honors society.

[52] According to the Daily Cal's website, "The *Daily Californian* is an independent, student-run newspaper published by the Independent Berkeley Student Publishing Company Inc. The newspaper serves the UC Berkeley campus and its surrounding community... Established in 1871, The *Daily Californian* is one of the oldest newspapers on the West Coast and one of the oldest college newspapers in the country."

Daily Californian staff.

lively gang of people. Paul Oechsli and I wrote a weekly column called "South of the Border" in which we analyzed Latin American news. Once we did a column on the Dominican Republic and the dictator at that time, Rafael Leonidas Trujillo. His representative in San Francisco, the Consul General, sent a letter to our editor denouncing us as Communists and demanding a retraction, which the editor tore up. But the Dominican Republic was known to have hitmen in the U.S. and Paul and I looked over our shoulders on dark nights.

At the *Daily Cal*, I met Jim Estes, another former GI who was one the editors, and we became lifelong friends. I fell in love with a young reporter, Wilma Rule, who fell in love with me too. We had sexy raucous parties in her apartment.

Life in the City

Jim Estes and I began to enter the San Francisco scene; the city was part of our lives. What can I possibly say about San Francisco that has not been said better and deeper that I can? It was the right time to be there. We were young, fresh out of the Army, and the city was intrinsically interesting. It kept reminding me of Rio. The ocean was a part of the city as it was in Rio. The streetcars were part of the scene as the *bondes* (streetcars) were in Rio.

We would go into the city when we could, but there was no BART train then. If we could catch a ride with someone or take the train we would. Jim would take me into the city with him on Friday night with ten dollars and we would return to Berkeley with nine dollars and some change on Monday after having been to the restaurants of the Far East and eaten all sorts of Chinese delicacies and Mexican foods. We favored one place that had a three-hundred pound barmaid who danced more gracefully than a feather. Sometimes we slept at the apartment of some dancers who performed at the Sinaloa restaurant, which featured authentic Latin American entertainment at 1416 Powell Street.

The city was soft and the people were friendly. One bar I had a fireplace and a quiet fire burning on those chilly nights that San Francisco can lay claim to. We used to think that Herb Caen's daily column of "Baghdad by the Sea" hit it perfectly: the lines of fog went up some streets like cat's paws.

We knew which Chinese restaurants gave out free soup. Beer was cheap at the bocce ball court, where the opera singing was great and they played a mean game of bocce ball there, too. Then we'd go to the Iron Pot[53] for breakfast. I spent an entire morning trying to make out with an attractive woman who at the end of two hours of hard work said that she was a lesbian (damned if I didn't always seem to be attracted to them).

We got ourselves a small sailboat, an 18-footer, and when the Pacific fleet came into San Francisco harbor we promptly sailed out to meet them. That is where I learned that there simply isn't any wind when you get in the lee of a huge aircraft carrier. They kept yelling at us to get the damn thing out of there. Well, we tried. With such happy thoughts in our minds we got back to classes each Monday.

Choosing a Thesis Topic

I wondered about my character in that a demanding professor would make me work harder. Other professors were great, but I

---

[53] The Florence Restaurant Iron Pot was located at 639 Montgomery Street. Its menu included this information: "The bohemian atmosphere here is strictly phony. For real bohemian atmosphere, go to Bohemia."

worked so hard for Prof. Sluiter that he honored me by making me his graduate assistant. He even asked me to give one lecture on Brazil for him. I am sure that every kid in the class hated me but I was on cloud nine[54].

You can imagine his consternation when I said that I would like to do my masters thesis on the 1930 Revolution in Brazil that brought Getúlio Vargas to power. Prof. Sluiter looked up over his glasses and protested mildly, "Mr. Young, this is not history, this is police reporting. The facts are not available yet. All you have is gossip." But after some grumbling he let me proceed with work on the thesis and I finished it in 1947. That thesis led me on many wild adventures in Brazil in 1949 and early 1950 - and the next 50 years. Because of Prof. Sluiter's high standards, I think my masters thesis was the best work that I did.

I rented a room in the house of a young psychology professor by the name of Daniel Levinson[55]. He had written a book called *The Authoritarian Personality* with Else Frenkel-Brunswik and two other researchers. He got his kicks in a strange way. Once, when Franny Crisswell ("Baby") was visiting me from Tacoma, Danny was having his bath and the bathroom was on the same landing as my room. He was enchanted with Franny and invited her in while his wife Maria soaped him up one side and down the other. In those days we didn't think anything wrong with that; it was interesting behavior but nothing more.

The first summer at Berkeley, a student named Noel Clad and I decided to hitchhike to Mexico City (hitchhiking was relatively safe in those days). We developed a game: we would size up the driver and guess whether he might have been an officer. Noel would sit in the front seat with him and compare notes. If we figured him for an enlisted man I would take over. One night in Texas we got picked up by some guy who asked how far we were going. He said he was just going "down the road apiece," but down the road apiece turned out to be Mexico City. Once there we found cheap lodgings in the red light district; the girls let us sleep during the day and at night they claimed the apartment.

---

[54] Prof. Sluiter died in 2001, after retiring from Berkeley in 1973. For a time he lived in Princeton as a visiting professor, living in my friend Mort Darrow's apartment.

[55] Daniel Levinson wrote his thesis on measuring ethnocentrism and was one of the founders of the field of Positive Adult Development while a professor at the Yale School of Medicine.

With my mother at graduation.

What Next?

While I was putting the finished touches on my 1930 Revolution study, a message came from the secretary of the graduate history department that Princeton University had received a five million dollar grant to promote research in Chile. The letter had been sent to all the universities with graduate departments in Latin American History. Each university was supposed to recommend their best student. I had specialized in Brazil but they asked me if I would be interested in the program anyway, even though it meant changing my specialization to Chile.

I said "Sure" and then was asked what my topic would be. That stumped me, so I interviewed every graduate student I could lay my hands on, asking them if they got a fellowship to Chile what they would research. The unanimous recommendation was a biography of Don Arturo Alessandri, a colorful, bombastic populist who had been President of Chile twice and was still alive. I wrote to Princeton, they accepted, and I received the first Doherty Foundation fellowship to Chile (as everything during that period had a Cold War twist, I suspect that the CIA wanted more specialists in Chile).

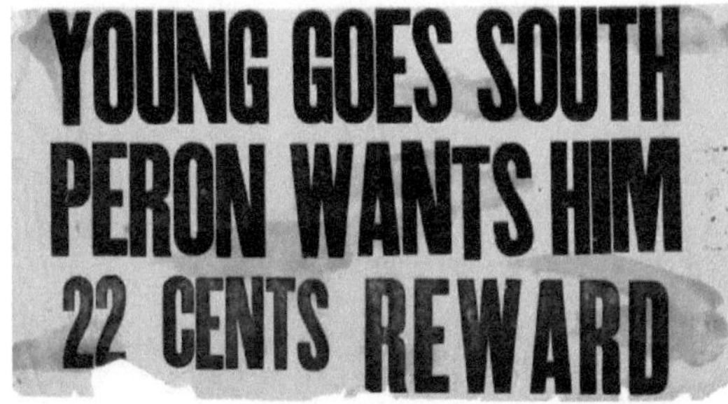
YOUNG GOES SOUTH
PERON WANTS HIM
22 CENTS REWARD

Helen Lee Wessel[56], who arranged the gift for Princeton, was a rabid Eisenhower supporter. She was very nice to me and was a fan and a personal friend of former president Alessandri.

The mail arrived with a check for $2,000 and instructions to get to Chile as fast as I could. I headed east to catch the Pan American World Airways plane from New York to Santiago, Chile, with a stop in Rio de Janeiro. I said goodbye to Berkeley, not knowing whether I'd ever see it or live there again.

[56] Helen Lee Wessel was the daughter of Henry L. Doherty, the founder of the Cities Service Oil Company (later Citgo) and of the foundation that made the grant.

Chapter 11. My Fellowship in Chile (1947-48)

In Manhattan, I went to the Pan American World Airways office in Rockefeller Center and bought a ticket to Chile with the money from the Doherty Foundation fellowship. I loved the excitement of going up to the counter and really buying a ticket, not just asking for some information, pamphlets, or brochures! To me, Pan American World Airways meant romance, excitement, and a sophisticated world that one only read about in magazines. I made sure I booked my flight so that I had to go through Brazil on my way to Chile. Belém and Rio de Janeiro were cities that had a special hold on my life and I had to go back. The glamour and appeal were still there.

I flew via Belém and tried to look up members of the old gang who had worked for Panair do Brasil and the SESP organization, but the world had moved on. I caught up with some of the girls from back in the day but for some reason the excitement was gone. I looked for Dionir but she had moved to Rio de Janeiro with her family. I flew on to Rio and drove past her apartment in Leme. I waved to some of her sisters who were on the balcony watching the cars go by, but I didn't see Dionir. I then flew reluctantly to Buenos Aires.

The years from 1943 to 1947 had seen momentous changes in the world, but Latin America did not change that much. I didn't know or like the city of Buenos Aires or the country of Argentina. I had been brainwashed by the Brazilians and unconsciously adopted

My parents and sister Annette seeing me off before I fly to Chile, 1948.

their attitudes when viewing the country. Though Brazil was an industrial giant when compared with Argentina, the Brazilians somehow felt that the Argentineans were the people with good manners and greater sophistication; Brazilians had the exuberance and Argentines had the sophistication.

I stayed for one day and then took a Pan American flight through the Andes. It was strange watching the mountains loom up and fly by on both sides of the plane. The pilots would find a gap between the mountains and fly through it, which scared the living bejeezus out of me. One is not accustomed to seeing mountains on both sides of an airplane as you're barreling along at 400-odd miles an hour. Finally we arrived in Santiago de Chile.

Margie Montague, now a civilian, was waiting to welcome me to Chile, although I hadn't seen her for the two years that I was at the University of California. Madigan General Hospital, Fort Lewis Washington, and UC Berkeley seemed far away and I decided to keep some distance between us. I simply couldn't feel this was just coincidence but did not know what to make of it.

Impressions of Chile

Chile was an adventure. I thought I knew Latin America – after all I'd spent almost three years in Brazil – yet I was totally unprepared for the Chilean experience. My experience of Latin America was of Brazil, and so in my mind Chileans clearly had to be like Brazilians. The first time I tried to give some Chilean friends a big Brazilian *abraço* (a big hug), I was promptly rebuked with a limp hand held out to shake. These were certainly strange people. They seemed cold at first, but the friends I made there were everlasting. They didn't speak mangled English as in Brazil; I felt like the village idiot once when I asked at a soda fountain, the way I had learned in Brazil, for a "milkee shakee." The man looked at me as if I was crazy and said did I want a milk shake – with all words pronounced correctly. I corrected myself sheepishly. The fact that I spoke Spanish with a Portuguese accent seemed to crack up all the students, but many of my female colleagues at the *universidad* ended up in bed listening to this quaint Spanish. I was an English-speaking gringo who mangled their Spanish enough to be understood – that was worth brownie points in the game of love.

Chile has the custom of taking eleven's or *onces*, a repast in mid-

Certifico que la impresión digito pulgar derecho, fotografía, firma y demás datos que figuran en este documento pertenecen al ciudadano don Jordan Martin Young

Prontuariado bajo el No 3060213 Santiago

Este número debe coincidir con el de la fotografía.

NOTA.—Este documento sólo acredita identidad. No acredita buenos ni malos antecedentes.

Serán consideradas como adulteraciones cualquier enmendatura o raspadura que se haga en este documento, así como también, las anotaciones no efectuadas por funcionario competente.

Esta cédula deberá ser renovada cada dos años. En caso contrario su poseedor incurrirá en las sanciones legales correspondientes.

Serie Sección

SANTIAGO IDENTIFICACION – CHILE 3060213

Firma del Interesado

Impresión Digito Pulgar Derecho

My Universidad de Chile identification card.

Jordan in front of a church in Farrellones, a resort town in the Chilean Andes.

afternoon like an afternoon tea, which carries them through to late, late dinners that often starting at 10 o'clock at night and roll on. Many an afternoon on the top floor of the Carrera hotel, which had a bar and swimming pool, I would prepare for the evening meal by having little sausages and pisco sours, a lethal, tart lemonade-like drink made from Chilean grape brandy.

Chile is a small compact country despite its length of over three thousand miles, all coastline, no interior. In *Chile: A Crazy Geography* the Chilean author Benjamin Subercaseaux described the impossible terrain of the country: "A nation sort of squashed in between the Andes and the ocean." If you made a left turn on the highway you would run into the Andes and if you made a right turn you would end up in the Pacific. Central Chile was the heartland in those days, with Santiago, the capital, and Valparaiso, the major seaport. Everything else was the boondocks.

Chileans had a degree of siege mentality. They were obsessed with the idea that the Argentines were either about to take some of their land in the southern lake region or were meddling in Chilean politics.

There were strange things in a strange country. Once while at a ski resort I stumbled into an inn way up in the Andes, almost the last inn before the Chilean-Argentine border. The innkeeper and guests were German-speaking Swiss. They had had a photo of Adolph Hitler stuck on the wall but that was just coincidence.

My sense of humor was very sophomoric: I thought that a joke about the beauty queen that won the contest in the city of Concepcion, thus being crowned Miss Concepcion, was the height of sophisticated humor. I dated an American girl for a while and took her to the soccer match one evening. Soccer is mostly a male thing and not many women go but Karen wanted to attend too so off we went. The first half was very exciting and we noted everyone going up the top row of the stadium, so we joined them. It was a magnificent sight – thousands of men peeing over the top of stadium, and the streams were golden arcs. Karen and I took one look and headed back to our seats a little bit wiser.

One of the odd things about Chile was the large Yugoslav population. They worked the coal mines of the country which ran out from the city of Concepcion, about 3,000 feet below the ocean. They were a strange bunch. Actually, everyone in Chile seemed to be mixed up with some branch of Europeans. There were Danish Chileans and German Chileans and Anglo Chileans. The Danish Chilean I choose to fall in love with had green eyes - she was named Elena Dalhgren. There were course some Chilean Chileans - all descended from the early Spanish aristocracy, or so they claimed. There were Basques who had impossible names with double rr's and double ss's, like Irrerrazeval and Underraaga. The *Rotos Chilenos*, "the Broken Ones," were the poorest people in Chile,and many looked partly Chinese.

Jordan with Elena Dahlgren.

A serious student in the center of Santiago.

I rented a small place near the American Embassy. They had no heat in the apartments in Santiago and God knows they could have used some. There was no central heating anywhere. The damp and cold of the winters was truly amazing. I found a beautiful substitute for central heating. I made do with a fellow undergraduate student who had the most statuesque body I had ever seen. I spent many an afternoon warming up when I was supposed to be hitting the books. I'm amazed that I ever got my thesis material collected.

It's funny how relaxed they seemed to be about sex in Chile. In this matriarchal society, the women seemed to be dominant. In a race to the bed the women would win. I met a lawyer one afternoon and before I knew it we were in bed in my apartment. She seemed to have a ball. She had enjoyed herself so much that she insisted that I come home with her and have dinner and meet her husband. Against my better judgment I agreed and never spent a more uneasy and unpleasant meal in my life. She, on the other hand, was cheerful as a Cheshire cat.

An aside about Irish-Chileans: Many Irish served in the empire of Spain because of their Catholicism. Indeed, the first president of Chile – which was part of Peru at the time - had the improbable name of Bernardo O'Higgins. He was the illegitimate son of the last Viceroy of Peru, whose name was Don Ambrosio O'Higgins. The Viceroy was not supposed to have any liaisons with native women, but he could not resist one beautiful Chilean woman. The net result was that they had a child, Bernardo. I'd seen many paintings of the man and one fine day when I lived in Princeton in the 1970s I got phone call from a man who identified himself as a descendant of Bernardo O'Higgins. He happened to live in New Jersey and he would like to make an appointment to see me. I said sure, come on over. He rang the bell one fine afternoon and I answered the door. I took one look at this guy and started to laugh. He was indeed the spitting image of O'Higgins. It was as if one claimed today to be the descendant of Abe Lincoln and looked just like him. He said he was interested in entering politics, and he was thinking of immigrating back to Chile. I suggested that it was not such good idea as the situation was getting tense in that country. I'll bet it was a CIA idea.

Chilean Politics

I worked as the ABC (American Broadcasting Company) radio correspondent and would send cables about impending revolutions and coups. One day in downtown Santiago I saw a crowd running down a street and naturally I joined them to see what all the excitement was about. Lo and behold the young air cadets had revolted and were firing at the crowd. This looked like a good story; I took out my press credentials and waved them over my head at the cadets. But damn if the next thing I knew a bullet whizzed over my head and I hit the sidewalk with a thud. The young soldiers were firing at me as I was waving my press pass. So much for press immunity!

The Chileans took their armed forces very seriously. The army had been trained by the Germans and it took me a while to get accustomed to their goose-stepping troops and German helmets. They had two armies in Chile when I was there: the regular army, which went about its business watching the Argentines, and the Carabiniers, which were a sort of police force. The latter had a reputation of being tough and you didn't want to fall into their hands. They were honest but no-nonsense. I never forgot the statement by a Carabinier general who said, "You don't want us in politics because our job is to kill people, and we are very good at it."

There were Communists in the Chilean government and society. The two had traveled a long road of accommodation since 1933, when there was the brief takeover of the Chilean government by Communists, but there was a "live and let live" mentality. There were Communists as Postmasters who were appointed by the federal government, and there were some mayors, but that was that. You did not put your gloves on when you shook hands with a Communist. Gabriel Gonzalez Videla, president at the time, seemed to be okay with the Communists but then later broke with the Communist Party. His break may have been one of those triumphs of the Cold Warriors in Washington.

Later, when Salvador Allende was elected president in 1970, the detente between the left and right broke down. I reflected that it was strange when the Socialists became the firebrands of the Allende government; he was unable to control forces on the extreme left and right wings that tore his administration to pieces and he was ousted after only a few years. In a move reminiscent of Mosaddegh in Iran in 1954, the CIA probably aided the right, which put Augusto Pinochet in power. How could this have occurred in Chile?

Working on My Thesis

I decided to attend classes at the Universdad de Chile. First I had to meet Professor Ricardo Donoso, who had been recommended by various professors at the University of California as a good resource person on Chilean history. I went to his apartment and there he delivered a withering blast at former president Alessandri, the man I planned to do my Ph.D. thesis on. Professor Donoso got excited and accused Alessandri of stealing the country blind and felt that he had ruined Chile while I listened,

A not so serious student and John Ellis, a graduate student who received another Doherty Foundation fellowship.

fascinated. After about an hour we bid goodbye and he wished me good luck on my topic.

I should have taken warning. Chile was a small country and Santiago an even smaller town. Everyone knew everyone and the gossip level was high. The next day I had scheduled a visit with the former President Alessandri. This was the first time I had ever met a president and I dressed accordingly, in my party suit. It went very swiftly: after I buzzed the door and he opened the apartment to let me in, he then coldly advised me that I had been talking to his political enemy and especially that *hijo de puta* Donoso. When he called Donoso a son of a bitch, I knew I was in trouble. Then he threw me out of his apartment. So much for former presidents. Needless to say I changed my topic to "Parliamentary Government in Chile from Balmaceda to Alessandri 1891 to 1924."

The most interesting classes I attended were on Saturday mornings down by the Mapuche River, where the law school met. The course was on the Chilean economy and taught by Professor Filipe Herrera. It was so cold in that damn classroom that the professor wore gloves and a muffler, and the students wore gloves as well. It was hard taking notes with your gloves on. The students were different from Brazil in that they paid no attention to me.

Travels Around Chile

I traveled with the students of Prof. Felui Cruz's class to Southern Chile and visited their lake region at Puerto Blest and Lago Llanquihue. The mountains looked so powerful and raw. It reminded me of the way I assume the Swiss Alps would look but since I had never been there I can't be sure. There were a group of Indians that cooked food in a pot in the ground and it was delicious.

What intrigued me most were the Araucanian Indians. They were strapping six-footers who took no nonsense from anyone. They were the only Indians that fought the Spanish to a standstill. I remember the awe and admiration that our history professors had for these fierce Indian fighters. The only way the Spanish conquered them was to roll barrels of whiskey down to their encampments until they were good and drunk.

I ran into them in the Temuco area, between Santiago and the lake region. I wanted to take a picture of one of the Indian women

Cóndor Station, Bolivia, the highest railway station in the Western Hemisphere.

who was wearing around her neck a beautiful silver neck piece. I took a photograph of it and the woman promptly became very angry and demanded five bucks for her photo. Reasonable enough, but I was a young graduate student and didn't have the money. She grabbed my camera, which was still attached to my neck, and started to pull while directing at me a string of curse words. When she called me a "Schweinhund," I gave up, paid two dollars, and asked where she had learned the German expression. It appeared that the German tradespeople in Temuco had taught the Indians how to swear.

My Trip to Bolivia

It was vacation time and I decided to visit northern Chile and its border countries of Bolivia and Peru. I managed to land an assignment from the ABC as a radio stringer. I got 50 bucks for five minutes on the air. I used to report revolutionary activity or that a revolution was about to break out every three or four days until they gave up on me. With those radio credentials, however, I received a pass and was entitled to a 50 percent discount on the airlines. I trotted over to LAN Chile and headed for the north to the town of Antofagasta, most of the way north toward the Peruvian border. The word itself sounded so silly that I kept rhyming words with it. There once was a girl from Antofagasta and

Indian women in Bolivia.

Street scene in Potosí.

so on.

I made friends with the pilots that flew the DC-4 plane and discovered that both were World War II veterans. The pilot was an Anglo Chilean and his copilot was a German Chilean, and both spoke flawless Spanish.

Flying north was a strange experience. I saw the designs made by the Nazca Indians, with crazy designs of monkeys and other animals etched on the mountainside. None of this could have been carved by people who only saw things from sea level. They needed elevation and plenty of it to get that perspective. Very strange. The desolation and moonscapes that I saw made me yearn for the soft warm Amazon.

I spent the night at a hotel across the street from the railroad station in Antofagasta and then took the narrow gauge railroad that plunged into the Andes to Potosí, Bolivia. Potosí was an old mining center that had a mountain of silver for which the town was famous. These railroads were really a tribute to the English engineers who built them. The cutbacks and switching around of the trains seemed almost impossible; switching back forth, we chugged into the Andes. We would go 20 miles and then switch back to rest up the engine and then proceed again. By night fall we had made some progress and I saw that it was going to be a cold night so I lay down in my cabin bunk with all my clothes on. It is odd how hot the desert is in the day time and how cold it is at night. Finally, I got to sleep, but woke up the next morning with my bones yelling at me that this was not the tropics. Ice had formed in the water pitcher in my small room.

I looked out the train window only to discover that we were surrounded by llamas. They are the most aristocratic looking animals I have ever seen. I sort of liked llamas in spite of the fact that they spit purple globs of glue-like subsistence and will not carry more than 50 pounds on their backs. If you put more on them they sit down and take careful aim at you and spit. Despite this they look so elegant that I always feel like taking them to tea at the Plaza.

We finally arrived in Oruro where I got a hot bath at a boarding house run by a Jewish couple and then continued on to Potosí. The mountain of silver worth millions of pesos had enriched Spain and taken thousands of Indian lives. What surprised me in this ancient town were the many gorgeous baroque churches which were now movie houses. It was fun to sit in pews, originally built for prayers, which had been turned into stalls and from which we watched John Wayne.

The town was cold and cheerless. One then understood the reason why the Inca worshipped the sun. You just felt miserably cold and damp. Walking down a street I heard German being spoken and whipped around only to discover that it was Quechua. That language has a lot of guttural sounds that I associated with German.

The mountain of silver at Potosí, Bolivia.

A group of drunken Indians made me join in a fiesta of some sort where I had to wave my handkerchief over my head and drink *chicha,* a local drink with a slight alcohol content that made me feel giddy. Only later did I discover that they made the drink ferment by spitting into it. Strange as it may sound I am still alive.

Potosí was a sad town and I was glad when I took the one-car train down to Sucre, which is the official capital of the country, and continued on the one-car track 4,000 feet down in almost a free-fall to Cochabamba, the California of Bolivia. That town was welcome as it was full of tropical fruit and warm sunshine, an oasis in the middle of Bolivia. From there it was a relatively quick and uneventful trip to La Paz. As I arrived at this 13,000 foot high capital I started huffing and puffing as I walked up a small flight of stairs. Even the airport worried us as the planes needed an inordinate amount of space to take off while the engines clawed the air for oxygen.

There was a beautiful secretary at the embassy and we became friends. We arranged to meet late in the afternoon at the apartment of a mutual acquaintance. I planned it oh so carefully. I remember that I got some good wine and what I thought would be good mood music that would set the tone. One of the records was "Cocktails for Two." I even had a pink oxygen tank by the bed which was supposed to lift you up. But how was I to know that the record was by Spike Jones with his zany remarks and hiccups and

Cochabamba, Bolivia.

that was the end of that little romance. I decided to leave for Lima, Peru.

On to Peru

The bus slowly climbed out of the hole that was La Paz and headed for Lake Titicaca. I used to joke with my friends that Titi was in Bolivia and Caca was in Peru. I think I got the boat at Guagui but I will not swear to it. The steamship was built on the spot by an Englishman, who then roughed it up with sections from the lowlands. It was built of steel and after a funny meal we went to sleep or tried to and awakened the next day at Puno in Peru. There I took another narrow-gauge railroad and passed what I thought was an Indian uprising. It turned out to be a Peruvian Independence Day celebration.

I got to Lima the same day. There must have been some benevolent god that watched over me as I ate whatever the Indians sold at the train stops, which meant meat pies and delicate pastries that tasted so light you wonder if they were in your mouth or not. But I never got dysentery. It was wonderful to see the women wearing these peculiar bowler hats which had been the latest thing in 17th century Madrid. Now the the specific style of hat indicated what town the people came from.

Lima was flat and soft and feminine. Women would sit and have tea at the Hotel Bolívar, which was called the snake pit. You could imagine the women hissing at some person they did not like.

Raúl Haya de la Torre, an old APRA (Alianza Popular Revolucionaria Americana) leader and opponent of the government, was under arrest and had taken refuge in some embassy. I tried unsuccessfully to contact him for an interview. In hindsight, I was glad I did not because it would have been considered a breach of his immunity and the police could then have gone in and arrested him.

There was a lot to see in Lima but someone suggested we go to Machu Picchu, the Inca city fortress that had remained undiscovered until Hiram Bingham stumbled on it in 1914. So off I went to Cuzco, the capital of the old Inca Empire. It was weird approaching the town of Machu Picchu. It was not there and all of sudden it was there. It was a walled city that was terraced and carried a strange air of a town that was not meant to be discovered.

I spent the night there and as there were no provisions for overnight guests I had to sleep in the workers' quarters. At sunset your imagination took off as the wisps of clouds floated in and out of the ruins and you could hear the strange conversations of Indians. I climbed Huayna Picchu, a nearby mountain, to view Machu Picchu from a distance. There were llamas all over the place and the buildings loomed over you. The stories that you could not slip a razor blade between the huge blocks of stone were true. The engineers who built this must have been magnificent.

Return to Chile

Back I went to Lima and then back to Chile. I was amazed at the animosity the Peruvians had for the Chileans. In the aftermath of the War of the Pacific (1877 to 1880), Chile had beaten up on Peru and Bolivia, acquiring rich copper mines, making Bolivia land-locked, and taking land away from Peru. The first books I used in the Chilean National Library had the imprimatur of the Peruvian National library stamped in the front.

There were some strange similarities between Brazilian history and Chilean history. The President of Chile, José Manuel Balmaceda, committed suicide as did Vargas - both over constitutional questions - one in 1891, the other in 1954. Both had parliamentary governments for a while.

My return to Chile was a long one. The plane in Peru only went as far as Arica on the Chilean border. I remember walking across the frontier between Peru and Chile and then got a ride to an airport in Chile where I got a flight down to Santiago.

Both before and after my return to Chile, I had really gotten into student activities. The government decided to raise the bus fares and the students decided to try and prevent this. We decided that the best course of action was to overturn buses, and student Young cheerfully joined in. Out on the streets of downtown Santiago, I learned that if you rock a bus long enough you can overturn it. It was great fun and I was getting a political education. The U.S. embassy called the next day and coldly reminded me that I was in Chile for a Ph.D., not to overturn buses. They must have had some paid informers or they would not have known so fast. I went to a political rally where we all shouted "*Abajo com el imperialismo Yanqui*" (Down with Yankee imperialism). My accent must have been pretty awful because a rumor swept through the meeting that there were FBI agents present.

A Chilean family took me to their ranch one Sunday. I had announced that I was from California so they assumed that I had grown up on a horse. The next day they invited to me to a paper chase. A paper chase? Not in my vocabulary. I soon learned about chasing paper over rails and jumping small ponds and galloping full speed ahead, chasing the "fox," a rider who left a trail of paper shreds. All I tried to do was stay on the horse and hang on to the saddle. It was of course an English saddle, no pommel like you had on a western saddle to hang on to. I ate dinner that night standing up.

Many a Sunday afternoon was spent hiking in the foothills of the Andes. I have Marjorie Montague to thank for these adventures. We would get a roast chicken and some white wine and just start walking. Once we came across some *huasos* (Chilean cowboys) practicing a small rodeo. A couple of cowboys would chase a heifer and try to throw her after by catching her by the tail, but the horses were supposed to do all the work. They all wore wonderful colorful clothes and were most friendly to us gringos. At night their serenades would keep us awake, as young men sang to their

Marjorie Montague, whom I'd met in the Army.

sweethearts at two in the morning strumming on their guitars.

Through the Straits of Magellan to Argentina

The U.S. Department of Education had scholarship grants for advanced research. One of the secretaries at the Embassy took a shine to me and told me about the program and asked if she could enter my name. I said sure, why not. I was awarded a U.S. Department of Education grant to proceed from Chile to Brazil by the fastest means possible to continue my work on the 1930 revolution. The money that they allocated for travel was something like $250 dollars, more than enough to fly from Santiago to Buenos Aires and proceed to Brazil overland. I calculated the money would be enough for a passage around the Straits of Magellan instead; since a ship was leaving soon, I grabbed it. The trip took some ten to thirteen days.

The ship was the S.S. Ravnanger on the Westfal Larsen line out of Bergen, Norway with a Norwegian crew and captain, but as we were taking the inland passage, which meant hugging the coast, we needed a Chilean pilot aboard. The ship was a small sturdy vessel carrying about 12 passengers. She plied a regular route from Bergen, around the bottom of South America to Santiago, back up to Buenos Aires, and then continuing up the South American coast to Norway once again. I picked it up in Valpariso, the port city for Santiago.

We left at midnight and headed south. It was odd to see the slender Chilean pilot beside the huge Norwegian hulk of the captain. The Pacific Ocean was on the outside and we threaded our way through the islands on the inside. As this was a small ship, we could range all over the ship and I loved to stand on the deck with the captain as we moved down south.

After two days we arrived in Valdivia and the captain said that there was nice bar across the street from where we were tied up. So a group of the English-speaking passengers drank a few pisco sours and then walked into town. There was a large square covered with linden trees and as we strolled around we kept hearing German spoken. Sure enough, these Chileans were all German immigrants.

We were a strange bunch on that boat. The man that really stands out in my in mind was the captain, a big burly hearty Norwegian type who kept slapping me on the back while I smiled bravely. I remember that we had lutefisk and drank a lot of aqua vitae on the trip, with the toast "*Din skol, Min skol a la vaca fica skol.*"

We continued going south and about midnight we reached Punta Arenas, the last large city on the South American continent. We had no cargo to deliver, so we would not dock but remained anchored off shore. The twinkling lights of the town looked so inviting but it was not to be. I was told that the tiny dots of light on the south side of our vessel were American oil rigs.

There, the captain said we had a few hours to explore the town and off we went. It seemed everyone was speaking German but the Chileans were unimpressed by this. I think it was Mt. Osorno that was a big volcano that loomed on the horizon. One of the fun things was to see the cargo being loaded on board the ship. The ship was old enough that there were rope-like containers. Maybe it was nostalgia but you watch the material being hauled aboard and stored in the hold of the ship. The stuff that was off loaded was as interesting as the material being put aboard.

We had reached the 46th parallel south which placed us near Antarctica. I kept my eyes open for icebergs but there were none to be seen. Around this point some Alacalufe Indians showed up. They seemed to be clothed in rags but it is reported that they also smeared their bodies with whale blubber and did not feel the cold. As their canoes approached our vessel we all leaned over the sides to greet them. Imagine our chagrin when they yelled for Ivory soap and Cokes.

The Straits of Magellan are relatively narrow and sudden storms would blow up and disappear in rapid succession. We left Punta Arenas and then a storm hit. Once the view was clear and in the blink of an eye fog and clouds set in. I was on the deck with the captain and the pilot when it began to sleet and snow. We slowly plowed ahead in the channel and, as it cleared up, we then raced for an opening in the channel. It abruptly closed with fog and started snowing again. The pilot, judging the width of the passage, decided to make a complete circle and by the time we came back to the original position the passage was open and we were able to proceed.

It was then that the pilot began to point out the submerged tops of the ships that had sunk in the channel. "That was a Japanese ship, that one was German, and there was one French ship." It was scary as we glided past the superstructures. By this time the storm had begun to get worse and the captain said that we were putting into a cove slightly to the left. "Throw out front and back anchors and put the search lights on. We'll spend the night there." The captain concluded, "I doubt if you are going to get any sleep tonight." Dinner was served with plates that had large magnets to keep them in place but it did not help. The tables and silverware went flying across the room. The captain came in to cheer us up but warned us to sleep with life belts on and be prepared for anything. All passengers were required to put on their brightly colored orange life vests. I was scared. What a funny thing I thought to drown in the middle of the Straits of Magellan in the 20th century. After all, Magellan made it through the straits and that was over 400 years ago.

Dawn finally came and it was a beautiful day with not a cloud in sight. We learned that an Argentine training ship had sunk during the night with the loss of all the cadets. We were a very quiet crew of passengers as we inched our way up the coast of Argentina to Buenos Aires.

The American cultural attaché was very angry when I appeared. He straightened his tie and said, "If you think I am going to pay a per diem for all that time you spent getting here on that ship instead of the 45 minutes flight from Santiago you're crazy." I told him not to worry and was informed that the cheapest way to the Brazilian city of Porto Alegre was by train. So off we went for what was the most unpleasant and disagreeable train ride I ever took. It shook the guts out of me. We went all over the map. When we passed Santana do Livramento and I was in Brazil again, my Chilean experiences were ended. I was never to return but the memories of a vibrant and democratic people would always stay with me.

Back in Brazil

The U.S. government grant for research in Brazil was only for three months. I started in Porto Alegre, which had been the seat of the 1930 Revolution. I checked into a hotel and paid my respects to the American Consul there, a man named V. Lansing Collins, Jr., who happened to be a Princeton graduate. He took great interest in my research and we promised to keep in touch with each other.

Rio Grande do Sul was the birthplace of Getúlio Vargas, who was currently living in exile in his hometown of San Borgia. I wrote to Vargas, telling him of my interest in the 1930 Revolution, and that I'd written a thesis at U.C. Berkeley on the subject. Much to my amazement, a letter arrived from Vargas a few days later, inviting me to his *fazenda* (farm) for a *feijoada* (a traditional lunch of beans and rice). I was thrilled with the letter, and promptly shared my enthusiasm with Consul Collins. To my surprise, Mr. Collins urged me to take caution in visiting Vargas, and said that he'd like to contact the American ambassador about my visit. I was surprised by all this but after all, the American government was funding my research grant in Brazil, so I figured I ought to oblige. A few days later, the ambassador wrote and said that he didn't think it would be judicious of me to go to the Vargas estate because Vargas had thrown his hat in the ring for the next presidential election. A visit by an American, he told me, would appear to outsiders as an example of the American government meddling in Brazilian affairs.

Crestfallen, I sent a letter to Vargas saying that I had asthma and would be unable to visit with him. That letter, much to my surprise, appears in Vargas' personal archives. I spent considerable time with a Dr. Spaulding, who gave me a valuable collection of documents concerning the 1930 Revolution. I also spent a wonderful afternoon with Erico Verissimo, a popular Brazilian author.

Content with my visit and my bag bulging with documents, I continued my journey to São Paolo and further investigations. What a shock when I arrived there. Everyone corrected me, saying that the revolution which I was researching was the wrong one, and they pointed me to 1932, when São Paulo had revolted against the Vargas government. Nobody felt that the 1930 Revolution was of any importance to the city.

After a month of fruitless research and investigation, I reluctantly left for Rio de Janeiro, but by this time I was weary and I wanted to return to the United States. I almost missed the plane out of Rio because I was stuck on the Pão de Acucar (Sugarloaf Mountain) for New Year's Eve (my flight was the next day). Unfortunately I didn't see Dionir during that brief visit.

Chapter 12. Princeton Graduate School (1950-52)

Arriving back in the U.S.A. in January 1950, I was breathless and eager to get back to California to resume my studies. A year in Chile and three months in Brazil had made me feel complete. I was getting on in years and would turn thirty that summer, so I checked in with my parents who were living in Flushing, New York, and bought myself an old 1940 Plymouth coupe to drive across the continent to Berkeley, California. All that activity took a total of three whirlwind New York days.

I also managed to pay a thank-you visit to Prof. Dana G. Munro, Director of the Woodrow Wilson School of Princeton University, as they had given me the fellowship to study in Chile. I was interested in how the other half lived - academics in Ivy League institutions, that is. We ate in the faculty cafeteria, which was then in the School's library. I was in awe of the huge tapestry that stretched over two floors tall.

An Offer from Princeton

Mr. Munro's assistant, a flamboyant Argentine specialist named Allison Bunkley, was there as well and we all chatted about the Latin America scene. I left for California after lunch. My Plymouth coupe made it to Berkeley and I heaved a sigh of relief when I arrived at the history department in Wheeler Hall. The faculty secretary greeted me with a big smile and said, "Welcome back and hey, you have a long distance phone call. Would you call operator 13 in Trenton, New Jersey and use the pay phone out in the hall? Thank you."

Dr. Munro was on the phone from Princeton with a weird offer. "Mr. Young, would you be interested in coming to Princeton and taking your doctorate here? I also need someone to be my assistant in the Woodrow Wilson School." I was flabbergasted to say the least and I remember blurting out to him, "What happened to Mr. Bunkley?" Dr. Munro, the consummate State Department diplomat, hemmed and hawed for a few seconds and then said simply, "There has been an accident and Mr. Bunkley is dead." My next serious and undiplomatic question was, "How did he die?" I was told that he was playing Russian roulette and blew his brains out.

Oh boy, I needed a few days to think this over. When I considered my future, Princeton had never been even mildly thought of. I'd just arrived that afternoon in Berkeley. If I accepted the offer, the stipend would be $2,500 a semester, the same as Berkeley. I liked Berkeley a lot. It was my milieu. It had San Francisco only a half an hour away. Princeton was only 50 miles from New York City and I would have my Jewish mother to contend with.

I spent a few days badgering people with the hypothetical question of what would you do if you were offered a job of this sort. I remember a professor who had just come from Princeton to California telling me, "Take the offer, because if you don't you will spend the rest of your life wondering if you made the right decision." I called after two days and told Dr. Munro that I accepted. I got back into the Plymouth, having never unpacked, and started back east across the U.S.A. to meet whatever destiny had in store for me. I have spent rest of my life wondering what would have happened if I had remained in Berkeley. (Talk about a personality split – I always felt that I had a California-type personality; by that, I mean at that stage of my life I could see myself married two or three times – a few children – some out of wedlock. That was California to me at that time.)

Somewhere along the road I picked up a hitchhiker who offered to split the gas costs. He turned out to be a pilot who had just the left the U.S. Air Force, was out of a job, and was about to be hired by the Israeli Air Force to shoot down Arab planes for $600 a week and a bonus for every plane downed. The first night we rented a motel room. He announced the next morning that I was a pretty trusting guy as he could have killed me and gone off in the car by himself. I gulped and for the next two nights I was quite nervous. He went as far as Trenton where he got out and I continued into Princeton. I arrived at two in the morning, and the Princeton police followed me to Dr. Munro's house. Princeton was such a small town that an out-of-state New York license plate was enough to invite suspicion.

Getting to Know Princeton

I will never forget my arrival at the Graduate College. A Gothic structure looming over me was my first run-in with Cleveland Towers. George the porter came down to help me unload my bags. (Yes, they had help in those days and lots of it.) I was a bit suspicious of George at first because fresh from Berkeley I felt he might just swipe my suitcases. But no, the master in residence had informed him of my pending arrival and he brought me into Suite 164 in the inner courtyard.

You must remember that my accommodations at the International House in Berkeley resembled a big closet. Here George first led me into a parlor with bay windows overlooking the Springdale Golf course, a huge fireplace, wood paneling, and a small bedroom. The only hardship was that one had to share the bathroom with the graduate students in the next suite, but they turned out to be a pair of nice Canadian topologists. I knew from beans what a topologist was but I would soon learn more.

As I was getting settled George announced that the master in residence would like to see me before dinner for some sherry. I wasn't quite sure what sherry was but I agreed to go. When he poured a tiny glass I belted it down in one gulp as we did in Berkeley. I later learned to sip sherry not gulp it, but about five gulps later, I began to feel merry and warm and decided that I was going to like this place a lot.

At this time, dinner was held in Proctor Hall under the paintings of frowning former deans and medieval gargoyles. We gathered at long tables and after a few moments someone would ask for silence and we would lower our heads to say grace in Latin. It sounded like "*Panema quo tedibonom da nobis hodia. Perdoum christem. Amen.*" I wasn't sure what it meant and, in the absence of sherry, whether I would last out the semester.

Jordan in Room 164 at the Princeton Graduate College.

We had to wear black robes over our shoulders. Several years later, the mathematicians put an end to that; when told that the black robes were regulation and had to be worn, they wore them with nothing else. There were no female graduate students so these hairy guys would swing into Proctor Hall with just the black shrouds flapping.

What else can I say about Princeton? First they decided they had to educate me. I was a whiz on Latin America. The senior faculty decided that I had all the information needed in that area but my knowledge on the European fields was weak and ancient history was nil. So they threw me to Professor R.R. Palmer who suggested that I take his course on the French Revolution and sit in on other professors that I thought I would learn something from.

Robert Arthur, a graduate student, showed how poor a judge of character I was. He snowed me under and I felt he would soon be in parliament, but I don't think he finished his degree. Jack Pole, another student, was the perfect Englishman with a pipe in his mouth so we could not understand a word he said. He later became the Regis Professor of American History at Oxford.

Otto Butz had the next suite and kept a lively place there. He became a politics professor at Princeton and edited a somewhat controversial book, *The Unsilent Generation*, in which his students wrote essays that refuted the notion that those who attended the university in the 1950s were apathetic.

We had Richard Hofstader, a visiting professor from Columbia University, give a seminar on the Progressive Movement. Another time I entered the hall leading to my suite and ran into a card pinned on one of the doors that announced that Charles Boxer had taken up residence there. Though primarily known as the local head of British army intelligence in Hong Kong prior to his internment by the Japanese, his book on the Portuguese in early Africa has been a pace-setter and an eye-opener for me. I knocked on the door and asked if he was the same man and he invited me in. He proved to be a damn nice guy. We had about five

Jordan with a group of Italian graduate students.

bourbons and wandered down to the Nassau Inn, where we decided to have a few more.

I thought a cocktail party for Boxer would be a nice idea but I hadn't realized that graduate students not only didn't give cocktail parties, but especially didn't invite their professors to such events. I did it anyway, inviting not only all the grad students I knew but all my professors. I couldn't understand Palmer's question about, "Would Emily Hahn be there?" until someone explained that Boxer had met this woman in Hong Kong, had a child by her before marriage, and then another child after marrying her. Hahn, however, had found married life too restricting and left England for an apartment in New York – which just might explain Boxer's presence in Princeton at the time. Hahn was quite a woman: the first female mining engineer graduate of the University Wisconsin-Madison and a member of the *haute monde* in Shanghai in the 1930s, she supported herself by writing for *The New Yorker*. She was a cigar smoking author of many damn good books. She told a story about Boxer, who was every inch the perfect English gentleman: reserved, discreet, fastidious, stuffy, and very English at home. But when he arrived in the Lisbon airport he would shed all these inhibitions and greet his friends with big *abraços* and slaps on the back that would have made any Latin proud of him.

There may have not been women in residence, but there were sure plenty around. The standard line was that a woman could not be seen leaving the Graduate College after 1 am. So we would move clocks ahead and plead with the girls: "You don't want to get me expelled from the University." The taxis would line up on the tarmac outside the GC after 1 am for the ladies. How often we smuggled food from our dinners up to our quarters to feed our starving women!

There was Mildred Demby, who moved in, literally, and she was determined to marry me. Though I told her up front, "no way," she did not believe it. We had the suite over the main entrance. It was noisy but nice. All of the goodbyes were heard as the arch over the entrance served as an echo chamber.

The Intellectual Excitement

The intellectual excitement was tremendous. You knew that you were being trained in an elite sense of the word. (I read Herman

Hesse's *Magister Ludi* and felt a great kinship with the novel.) The seminars were quite demanding. One that I never forgot involved a student (Howard Edelman, who became a distinguished professor at CCNY) and a professor who was the world's leading authority on the Roman Empire snarling at each other: "Okay, let's look at the papyrus and see who is right and who is wrong."

Buzzer Hall was a famous professor, but I never caught any of his lectures on Garibaldi until his last years, when five other instructors and I had to precept for him in his course on modern European History, a course which was built around historical novels. The way in which novels could show a person's daily life and emotions in a way that textbooks couldn't, lasted with me and changed the way I taught.

The eating tables were interesting in that you generally gathered with your own discipline. Historians sat together, mathematicians sat together, physicists sat together, and English department people clustered among themselves. But if you came in late you sat anywhere and that is where the great conversations began. Two students that I ate with became ambassadors: Koichi Komura who became the Japanese ambassador to Brazil and reappeared later in my life, and Pablo Valdes, who became the Chilean Ambassador to Morocco.

I liked the atmosphere of the precept. It was made up of eight or ten students who had to read the assignment and listen to the senior professor lecture; this was followed by banter around the room. I'd ask a student a question and most of the time he would fob it off to some other student who had read the stuff and say, "Hey that's a good comment. What do you think, Frank?"

Professor R. R. Palmer's seminars on French history were superb. In particular, the one on historical evidence was both grueling and thorough. It usually turned into a bloodbath for students who did not prepare for the work he demanded. We were taught to believe nothing unless we saw enough evidence, both written and unwritten, to make up our minds. This "historian as a detective" method caught my fancy. This seminar was where I met the future diplomat Charlie Stout, who a became a lifelong friend although he was a casualty of Palmer.

Another excellent course was Frank Craven's history of Virginia. The best deal was America Castro, the Emory L. Ford Professor of Spanish, who lectured on the great Portuguese epic writer Camões. I was so scared I never opened my mouth, as guys like Jack Hughes and others gave deep opinions about the soul of the Spaniards. What did I know about Spain?

The history department did come up with one truly disastrous idea: they would teach us how to teach. This seminar was led by Professor Gordon Craig, who went on to become a German historian at Stanford. He told us never to turn our backs to the students, even when writing things on the board. Maybe it was his combat experience, which meant we might be shot in the back by students. He was a former Marine and those tactics wouldn't work on us. Above all he emphasized the importance of speaking clearly. We had so many things on our minds that we politely and impolitely ignored him. It was only later when we were out in the real world that we tried to recall some of his words of wisdom, but on the whole it was a colossal failure.

After one semester I was elected to the House Committee of the Graduate College. That cemented my decision to stay at Princeton for my doctorate. For this vague honor, I had to say grace in Latin on Tuesday night before dinner.

I liked the atmosphere of arranging the Wednesday evening speakers program. It was amazing to discover the number of people who would pay their own way to Princeton for the honor of talking to the Graduate College. I was especially interested in Alceu Amoroso Lima[57], a prominent Brazilian journalist and Catholic activist; his writings on theology were of considerable interest to Brazilians at the time, but apparently not to Americans in attendance. William F. Buckley, who had just published *God and Man at Yale*, so packed the hall that we had to open the windows; people were actually listening from outside, but I never could figure out why. And so, for balance, I invited W.E.B. du Bois. Du Bois was angry at the U.S.A.; we were in the middle of the Korean War, which he did not support. He gruffly told me he would not accept my invitation to dine but rather he would arrive at Princeton Junction at 7, speak at 7:30, and leave as soon as it was over, catching the next train out. The audience was indifferent and even

---

[57] Alceu Amoroso Lima was one of the founders of the *Movimento Democrata-Cristão* (Christian Democratic Movement) in Brazil, writing under the pseudonym *Tristão de Ataíde*. In his later years, he opposed authoritarianism in general and Fascism in particular.

slightly hostile. I also invited Rudolph Bing, the director of the Metropolitan Opera, who sent me a season ticket with a box seat attached to it.

When you left Princeton you felt that you had been educated. We were a small school with only a maximum of several hundred graduate students. We thumbed our noses at Harvard and Yale. They were both factories.

Married Life

I had not been in contact with Dionir, the woman I had met in Belém, for nearly seven years. Suddenly she reappeared in my life in February 1950. She had been in a long-standing romance with a powerful congressman and banker in Brazil named Oswaldo Carvalho Costa. He'd given Dionir an apartment and hired her brother-in-law as his private secretary in an effort ensnare her through her family, but Costa was married and it didn't appear that he would ever marry her. He said that he had gone to the Pope and had his marriage annulled, but Dionir knew he was a womanizer. She didn't want to marry a man like that.

Dionir wrote me a letter and addressed it to my parents. My mother called me in Princeton to tell me there was a letter from a young lady I had known in Rio de Janeiro, and she sent the letter to me. I was puzzled to receive it after all those years. The letter said that she was coming to the U.S. with her sister Oceanira and her brother-in-law, Alberto Kronsfoth, for two weeks and hoped to see me. I was intrigued and responded immediately that I'd be happy to see her to bring closure to our friendship. But it awoke something in me - the flame was still burning.

I arranged to meet her at her hotel in New York, the Gladstone. I walked into the lobby eagerly with my jacket wide open and her first words were (in Portuguese) "Button your jacket!" I should have known then that a marriage with her would never work (after 60 years the jury is still out).

I invited her to Princeton and began to squire her around. The fire was rekindled and I asked her to marry me. She refused. A telegram arrived that Oswaldo's plane had crashed near Rio. We all assumed that he had died. She told me, "I have to return to Brazil to close out my affairs and find out whether Oswaldo is dead or alive. I'll come back and marry you." I didn't believe a word of it and didn't think she'd come back.

Much to my surprise, three weeks later, she appeared once again in New York. Oswaldo was alive but injured, and she had broken off her affair with him. I brought her to Princeton. When I told my parents I was going to marry a Brazilian, my father asked, "Is she black?" and I said, "I never looked!"

Dionir rented a room in a house on Nassau Street near the university. One day an FBI agent appeared at the house looking for information regarding Jordan Young. Apparently Oswaldo had appealed to the chief of police in Rio de Janeiro and used his friendship to make the inquiry in the U.S.; apparently, he wanted to check up on me. That was the last we heard from the FBI or from Oswaldo.

Outside our first house at "The Barracks."

I suggested that we get married on May 10th. We didn't want a church wedding, so we got married by Justice of the Peace John Cheeseborough of the Borough of Princeton, N.J. We moved to 224A Marshall Street in the Butler Tract (a.k.a. The Barracks), University housing that had been built for the war years and remained as a permanent home for married graduate students, since you couldn't live with a spouse at the Graduate College.

This was not a luxury house. We decided to paint our

unit and my Brazilian bride thought it was a quaint custom. The green paint from our spraying machines filled the air and we drank and breathed the stuff; this was all well before the EPA. We bought a $7 sofa from fellow students with the proviso that they would help me carry it to our unit. A vanity table went for $3.50 and we borrowed a bed and rug from my family. We settled in like old married people and my Brazilian wife took to Princeton life like a duck to water. The first time it snowed she called me at the office and asked if could I please come home immediately. I told her not to worry and that graduate assistants did not go flying home just because it was snowing.

Our unit was located at the end of three units; one thin wall separated us from our neighbors. It seemed that sex had a high priority for us all because the amount of sexual activity was tremendous. It appeared that we were all just married and did nothing else. A political science couple (I think his name was Dankwart Rostow) finally moved their bed into the living room. They made so much noise we could not talk or think. The straw that broke the camel's back was when Dionir awoke with what I thought was a fit of coughing in the middle of the night. I got up and brought her a glass of water. She refused the water and we figured out it was the woman in the next bedroom.

Mort Darrow, who became a lifelong friend, also lived in the Barracks but not near us. He later became vice president of Prudential Life Insurance, but he and his wife Maureen never succeeded in killing the rat that stuck his head out the hole in their ceiling in the Barracks.

Dionir and I decided to go to the Carnival Ball at the Waldorf Hotel - now that was an operation. We wrote to the folks back in Rio and they managed to get Dionir a feather costume made up from the plumage of some of the rarest birds in the Amazon. Would the conservationists raise a stink today! And correctly so, but that was then and now is now. We were so pleased with the costume that I had Dionir try it on. She stood up on the kitchen table in all her plumaged glory and just as I was admiring her I saw an anthropology graduate student passing by the window and shaking his head in wondrous amazement. He clearly felt that Dionir had returned to her origins.

Dionir learned to be a good cook, even though she had never cooked in Brazil - it was on the job training. Word got out among the graduate students and invariably they would show up about dinner time and we would make another place at the table for them. We even put a notice on the Graduate College bulletin board that if anyone was alone around Christmas to come on over and join us. Mary Ann and David Wishart, Betty Kingseed, and an African student appeared one year.

Dionir in her feathered Carneval costume.

The Colloquium on Luso-Brazilian Studies

In October 1950 the Library of Congress and Vanderbilt University pulled together the leading authorities on Brazilian studies from the U.S., Portugal, and Brazil. Many met for the first time at the conference in Washington, D.C., called the International Colloquium on Luso-Brazilian Studies. As an up-and-coming Brazilian scholar, I was invited to attend.

Jordan in his gaucho Carneval costume.

The colloquium stressed cultural anthropology, linguistics, fine arts, literature, instruments of scholarship, and history. I had been going to New York to take a course from Professor Bailey W. Diffie of CCNY, and he presented one of the papers, entitled "Bibliography of the

Principle Published Guides to Portuguese Archives and Libraries." The attendees expanded their views and promised to stay in touch in the future. I met Alexander Marchant, a distinguished professor of Brazilian history, at the conference. I came away from the conference with my mind boggled at the possibilities of research and writing about Portugal and Brazil.

Meeting Albert Einstein

The stay in Princeton would not be complete without the inevitable contact with Albert Einstein. My wife especially demanded an audience with him. I confabulated with the graduate math students; Jim Mayberry told me that a station wagon that left from Palmer Square at 10:30 am picked up Einstein in front of his house. The station wagon then continued on to the Institute for Advanced Studies, which was located on the outskirts of Princeton. We planned to rendezvous the next day at 10:25 so that we could take the back seat of the station wagon and thus have a commanding view of whoever entered.

My wife got herself all dressed up in her Sunday clothes, explaining that it was not every day you met Einstein. I tried to explain that we might not even see him but if she wanted to get all spruced up it was okay with me and Jim Mayberry. We were the first people at the bus and scrambled aboard. As predicted, the station wagon started down Nassau Street and turned into Mercer Street where Einstein lived. By that time we had picked up two other passengers - one took the front seat and the other the second row. When we got to Mercer Street, Einstein wasn't anywhere to be seen - we stopped a moment and then moved on. The driver had his schedule to keep and Einstein or not he was keeping to the schedule. A little further down the block we noticed Einstein walking and came to a screeching halt to haul him aboard. He sat right in front of us and some poor graduate student who was frightened out of his skin sat beside him.

Albert Einstein looked like God was supposed to look like. He was dressed in baggy grey trousers and sneakers without stockings. It was summer and he was wearing a shirt with a sleeveless sweater. My wife was studying the contour of his head - the face as much as she could see of it - and his hands. He had the look of a tired angel. His hair was a silken white and over that he wore a nondescript hat;

I was afraid my wife might snip a lock off his hair but she restrained herself. Like a good Brazilian, however, she could not resist mentioning to me that he ought to take his hat off, as there were ladies in the car. She continued giving me her impressions of the great man as we went along in Portuguese.

When we got to the Institute, Einstein got out first and made sure to hold the door for my wife and gave her a gracious smile. Di almost dropped dead. Our mathematician friend assured us that he never held the door for anyone. We figured out that he understood Portuguese and always appreciated a pretty woman.

Another mathematician at the Graduate College at the time was John Nash, about whom the book *A Beautiful Mind* was written. I heard that when people were playing a game of Go in the common room, Nash would come along, look at the Go board, and kibitz, telling people where to move.

Finding a Job

The day came when Professor Munro told me to finish my thesis or else. I knew what that meant. I'd been dawdling too long and not getting the damn thing written. Dionir announced at the same time that there were two women living in 224A Marshall Street and one of them was going to leave in June - either I would finish up the thesis, or she would leave. (We've since discussed, many times, whether I would have finished it without her push. I was studying there before she appeared. Be that as it may, I did finish it.)

I was astonished to find that the job market had dried up, so I began interviewing for various nonacademic jobs – such as Becton Dickenson, a medical equipment company, and Chase Bank.

Chapter 13. Investment Banking in Brazil (1953-55)

At the Chase Bank office in New York, a Mr. Westmore Wilcox interviewed me on the 23rd floor of the Chase Bank and turned me over to a Mr. E.G. Burland. He decided that I might be useful to them in an investment banking firm that they were planning to open in Brazil. Though I had never had any economics or mathematics classes, I wasn't daunted, and they didn't seem to be either. They said they had two hot shot Wall Streeters, George Washburne and Dick Aldridge, whose cousin was Nelson Rockefeller. And of course Eugene Black Jr., who really wanted to be a playwright, but his qualification was that his father ran the World Bank.

Washburne and Aldridge were the two guys who knew Wall Street and I knew Brazil. They would marry us and all would be well for Chase. It was, however, a marriage made in hell, as we discovered later. The company would be known as Interamericana de Financiamento e Investimentos S.A. I would have a *mil reis* salary (that is, in the Brazilian currency), and I would start in October.

Back to Rio

We took a cargo ship with the Moore-McCormack Lines headed for Rio. We were held up in port in New York before we left because a union leader had disappeared and they suspected the Mafia was hiding the body somewhere in the hold of the ship.

The first mate greeted us as we came aboard and asked casually whether we played bridge. We said that we did not and he grimly said, "You will before you leave." So started a twelve day trip that was my return to Brazil, and we did know how to play bridge by the

Dionir trying on a life a preserver for the trip to Rio.

time we left the ship. So did everyone else, including an Australian woman who asked to be "knocked up by the Captain," as she did not want to miss the view of harbor of Rio. When the morning came for our arrival she was beaming at everyone as we had coffee and said that the Captain had knocked her up and the first mate had knocked her up and even Mr. Young had knocked her up. I can't believe she didn't know how we used the word back in the U.S.A.!

Returning to Brazil in 1953 as an investment banker trainee with a newly minted Ph.D. from Princeton under my arm was certainly a new twist in my life. It was going to be on-the-job training as I had no strong knowledge of economics, or math, or anything else that would prepare me for this job other than knowledge of Brazil. This was my first commercial job and I entered the assignment with the highest of hopes. I always wanted to make a million dollars and investment banking seemed to represent the right road to such wealth.

The New Bank

Our new bank was a subsidiary of the Chase Bank of New York and the International Basic Economy Corporation (IBEC), which was founded by Nelson Rockefeller in 1947 to help developing countries establish home-grown companies. We were to provide technical assistance and financial capital for the economic development and diversification of Brazil. Our job, along with IBEC, would be to develop Brazil's capital market by underwriting and distributing securities within the country. I was part of one of the most powerful financial institutions in the world.

Brazil was just getting into the modern capitalist world. Though Getúlio Vargas had been out of office since 1945, his return to politics and his presidency in 1951 worried a lot of people. Vargas continued with his populist gestures and was determined to industrialize Brazil. The business world, especially within the U.S.A., didn't know how to read Vargas. My personal opinion was that his biggest sin was not being anti-Communist enough for the CIA. Why Chase Bank and David Rockefeller decide to venture into Brazil with an investment firm of this nature is an interesting question[58]. They may have been willing to learn and getting their feet wet was the only way. Brazil was capital-short and the Brazilian elite had no confidence in their own country; whenever possible they would put their money in Miami real estate or buy dollars. It was difficult to get Brazilians to invest in their own companies.

I learned after only a brief acquaintance with Latin America that economic growth there was lagging due the lack of medium- and long-term credit for equity financing. While there were a few *financeiros* that channeled private funds into new enterprises, merchant or investment banks, such as those found in profusion in Europe and the United States, simply did not exist. Besides the field of government bonds, capital markets capable of underwriting security issues were completely absent.

North American and European banks compounded the problem because they rarely extended credit for more than three months, and only for traditional activities. It was an area of real frustration for Latin American entrepreneurs who wanted to expand and diversify their businesses but lacked the capital resources to do so. Here was a glittering opportunity for Chase but we had to find our way around a legal obstacle before we could proceed.

The Glass-Steagall Act of 1933 prohibited U.S commercial banks from participating in domestic investment banking. They could do so overseas through the provisions of the Edge Act of 1919. Chase had an Edge Act corporation but had used it solely as a real estate holding company for branches in Paris and the Far East.

---

[58] David Rockefeller's *Memoirs* (New York: Random House, 2002) describes Chase Bank's entry into Brazil.

Chase amended the charter to permit investment banking and created our new subsidiary, the Interamericana de Financiamento e Investimentos S.A. as a joint venture with IBEC to underwrite and distribute securities within Brazil. We recruited fourteen of our Brazilian correspondent banks to join us as shareholders and we launched the new company in 1952.

Interamericana did well during its first two years of operation, but then hit a snag when the Brazilian economy fell into recession. We never recovered our momentum. Pressure built from the home office to cut our losses and despite our pleas to correct the problems and wait for better days we lost the fight in 1956 and Chase sold its shares of Interamericana to IBEC.

In retrospect I have no doubt that the concept underlying Interamericana was sound and the Brazilian partners were among the strongest banks in the country. Unfortunately, few at Chase had any interest or sympathy for the idea. We needed first-rate investment bankers to run it and enough time to prove the idea could work. Even though several bright young junior officers were assigned to the project we never found an experienced senior banker to head the operation.

Ironically, after Chase gave up on Interamericana, IBEC converted it into a mutual fund, Fundo Crescinco, the first of its kind in Latin America. Most of our Brazilian partners rolled over their investment into the new company, which proved to be enormously profitable and still exists today. Many of our original Brazilian partners created their own investment banks - a further indication of the validity of our original concept. Sadly, Chase had fumbled a major opportunity.

Office and Home

George Washburne was the chief executive of the organization. Apparently he was very good on Wall Street but had little interest in how Brazil did things. The second in command was Richard S. Aldrich, Nelson Rockefeller's cousin, who was supposed to handle the firm's operations in São Paulo. The third officer was Eugene R. Black, Jr., ., whose father ran the World Bank. And then there was Jordan Young whose only assets were knowledge of Brazil and a Ph.D. from Princeton University.

Life had its serious moments as I learned the investment banking business. I never had any formal business experience and all this was new to me, but I got to work on time and tried to look busy. My immediate boss was Antoine Forat. He was so suave and so French. Then there was Vladimir Jednov, a Russian by way of China, and Cesare Pougy, from a good family. The first thing they taught me was how to write a prospectus.

Our office was on Avenida Rio Branco at the corner of Avenida Getúlio Vargas, smack in the middle of downtown Rio de Janeiro. Candelária, a stodgy old church, was just around the corner. I loved downtown Rio. The Rua dos Mercadores, one of my favorite neighborhoods, was right out of colonial Portugal. It had little narrow streets that wandered toward the bay.

We lived in Leme, a lovely enclave right at the end of the Copacabana beach. All the traffic for downtown Rio turns off at Avenida Princesa Isabel. We had our apartment on the second floor right over the Taberna Atlantica.

I enjoyed the apartment because it was on the beach. At night we could hear the pounding of the waves as they hit the sand. In 1953, Avenida Atlantica was a narrow two-lane street. The south Atlantic Ocean was just yards away, and the spray from the ocean waves would make everything wet and damp in our apartment. There were two little islands off the coast which were sort of beacons, flashing a green and red light at night. Cargo ships that were heading out to sea would always ply their way between those two tiny pieces of land. There is something very romantic about a squat dingy freighter plowing through the open Atlantic.

Some days I would come home at lunch from the office and go swimming in front of the house and then go back to work. I would signal the maid to bring my lunch out to the beach by waving a towel. If I ever felt like a pasha it was then - sitting on Copacabana Beach and signaling for my lunch.

My Professional Work Card

In a carryover from the Vargas dictatorship of 1930-1945, Brazil was still very much a bureaucratic and corporatist state. Things didn't just happen, and everything was supposed to be organized. Brazil did not become a democracy because the army decreed it; it would take the country many years before it would shed the image of a fascist state as well as a corporate one. You needed stamps on every document, and you needed documents for everything under the sun. You needed official papers to start up or end a company, papers with stamps were necessary to prove you were a citizen, working papers were required of every person, and so on. As Americans, we tend to forget how little the Federal government or the government at any level intrudes in our private lives. That possibly was the hallmark of American civilization: you were left alone to do whatever you wanted to and in any way you wanted to do it until the destruction of the World Trade Center in 2001.

I was sent out into the street to sell the stocks we were issuing, but before that I was told that I had to join the bankers union. All the unions were semi-governmental organizations. I found that 416 *cruzeiros* were deducted from my salary check every 15 days to go to the IAPTEC, which was the Bank Clerks Institute of Social Security, but this could only happen after I got my professional working papers. As a foreigner I had to have a piece of paper called Immigration Registration Card Model Number 19, which proved that I was in Brazil legally. I slowly worked my way through that labyrinth.

I was then permitted to obtain my professional work card (number 58196) and I was fingerprinted and handed my own ID. This was in the form of a little passport stamped on the outside with the words National Department of Labor and the seal of Brazil and the words *Carteira Profissional.* I now had a professional work permit[59], although why I had to have a professional working

---

[59] Page one of my work permit contained articles 13, 29, 30, 36, 55, 375, and 376 of the law dated May 1,1943, which came under decree law 5452 of the Vargas Dictatorship. This, however, was 1953 - but not to argue. The next page had a chatty note from someone called Alexandre Marcondes Filho telling me that this little identity book was a picture of my life and at a glance one could see how many jobs I held or how restless I had been. There was room for all the relevant facts like height, weight, color of eyes, and any identifying marks. It was recorded that I was the son of Irving and Frieda Young and that I was born in the U.S.A. on Sept 20, 1920. It indicated that I was married and had a secondary education. I was listed as an office worker and there were ten spaces for the number of Brazilian children I had. Page 7 took care of my work contract, number of people in the organization, and my salary. Pages 8 through 18 were reproductions of the work contract. The sum of 416 cruzieros was indicated as my contribution to the union, which was not named. Vacation and union dues were treated on pages 19 to 29. Pages 29 to 47 demanded to know what work accidents I had and then official signatures from the company I worked for.

identification card I will never know. I thought I was finished with paperwork.

I was now a full-fledged member of the union and would receive all the medical benefits and therefore I had to be examined by the union doctor. I balked at that, and so every three months I received a notice until I capitulated and was told to report to the Ministry of Labor, 14th floor, room 1440 at 4 p.m. I fortified myself with two gin and tonics and arrived at the examination office to find 14 people ahead of me. Dr. Ruy, the examining doctor, was never able to see me because time ran out. I clutched all my documents and stalked out the door never to return, but I had my work papers.

The Company

The Board of Directors of our company included, except for the two North Americans, what seemed like the best Brazil had to offer at that time. They were as follows:

- Barão de Saavedra, Director, Banco Boavista
- Ernesto G. Fontes, President, Banco Portguês do Brasil
- Theodoro Quartim Barbosa, Director, Banco Comércio e Indústria de São Paulo
- Charles Emmet Waddell, Director, Anderson Clayton
- George Washburne, Director, Superintendente Interamericana
- Richard S. Aldrich, Director, Gerente Interamericana

The following banks (in addition to The Chase Bank of New York and International Basic Economy Corporation) were listed as shareholders in Interamericana. They were considered the cream of the Brazilian banks of the period. Not a single one exists today (August 2006) under the same name. The list exhibits the profound changes that have occurred in the banking industry of Brazil in the past 50 years.

- Banco Boavista
- Banco Português do Brasil
- Banco Comércio e Indústria de São Paulo
- Banco Moreira Salles
- Banco Comércio Indústria de Minas Gerais
- Banco Mercantil de Niterói

- Banco Mercantil de São Paulo
- Banco Nacional do Comércio de São Paulo
- Banco da Província do Rio Grande do Sul
- Banco Sul Americano do Brasil
- Banco Brasileira Para a America do Sul
- Banco da Bahia
- Banco Comercial do Estado de São Paulo
- Banco Econômica da Bahia

The entire operation was under the jurisdiction of the SUMOC (*Superintendência de Moeda e Credito*, or Directorate of Money and Credit) which was created in 1945 with ample powers to supervise the banking system. The direction of the Bank of Brazil was included in its mandate. It was run by six officers headed up by the Minister of the *Fazenda* (Secretary of Treasury). SUMOC operations were always complex because SUMOC representatives, Bank of Brazil operatives, and Department of the Treasury personalities had different agendas. The resulting stalemate often forced the President of the country into the decision-making process. Brazil apparently had no laws covering capital markets.

Dênio Nogueira, a Brazilian economist who received a degree from the University of Michigan, did not look favorably upon our work. At the time he was editor of the *Conjuntura Econômica*, the journal that spoke for the government. (I was later was the American representative of the magazine.) After the 1964 revolution, he became head of the Central Bank. In 1954, however, he felt that we at Interamericana should help the Brazilians write the rules for the stock market and if we screwed up it'd be bad news. In fact, we did write the rules and it was bad news, and I've heard that he felt we should have been run out of the country for screwing up so badly.

Our Products

Our first prospectus was fascinating. Tacked onto the front page was the fact that Deltec, an investment house run by a smart U.S. businessman by the name of Clarence J. Dauphinot Jr., had joined us on one offer. Deltec could run circles around Interamericana. They had street smarts and we did not.

We issued the following stocks:

- Redimix Concrete
- General Tire and Rubber Company
- Arno Indústria e Comércio (domestic appliances)
- Mannesman Steel
- Brinquedos Estrela (children's toys)

There was a struggle over what to do with these and other potential stock issues. The tug of war was between seventy-year-old E.G. Burland, an old fashioned, no-nonsense type of investment banker who employed me, and thirty-five-year-old George Washburne as to how far and how fast they ought to proceed. Burland, a cagey New York banker, was cautious and he said he could not feel the situation. He'd hired me and sent me to Rio de Janiero. I was in the wrong camp; George Washburne quickly eased Burland out of the picture and decided to go full speed ahead. I was soon on my own and George Washburne didn't know what to do with me.

Burland was correct. The Brazilians would not, or could not, supply the necessary capital to these issues and most were underfunded and never took off. Brazilians were very cautious with their money if it was not a sure thing. The stocks were all duds and no one on the street would touch them.

I was put on the selling end and found that this was as good a way of learning about the investment banking business as any. This was the way the older Eugene Black, who headed up the World Bank, learned the trade and his son was now in our firm. His son, however, wanted to write plays. I found that I was selling about 2 million cruzeiros ($47,619 in 2013) worth of stock a month. I got a raise and now was earning 15,000 contos a month or - are you ready for this - a grand total of $300. Hell, I did better with SESP when I was giving out anti-malaria pills to the Amazon rubber workers ten years back.[60]

I often went to the stock exchange at 2 in the afternoon. The reason I went so late was that the stock exchange opened at 2 p.m.

---

[60] The *cruzeiro* was the currency of Brazil from 1942 to 1986 and again in the 1990s. The first version, the *cruzeiro antigo*, circulated from 1943 to 1967 until it was replaced by the *cruzeiro novo* at a rate of 1000 *cruzeiros antigos* = 1 *cruzeiro novo* because of high inflation. A *conto* was 1,000 *cruzeiros*. One current (2013) dollar is equivalent to about 42 1953-style cruzeiros.

and closed at 2:20 and there wasn't much to do. It was like an old club. I would walk across the trading floors and chat with the various brokers, most of whom I knew. We'd offer a bid for our stock and flag the price up until someone bit and bought several thousand and then we'd withdraw our support and the stock would sag.

Someone at the office had the bright idea that we ought to sell some of the Brazilian Treasury Bills that we owned. They gave me the job. I was supposed to sell over $100,000 worth of these bonds. I was told to inquire about the going value, or street value, of the bills and to announce that we might have them to sell. I wandered around the stock exchange asking various brokers for advice and thus alerted the entire brokerage community what was going on. By asking around I drove the price down about 5 points and ultimately we lost a lot of money on the deal. I dreaded seeing the year-end report with a loss of over $100,000. I now learned a lesson in creative accounting: the loss wasn't there. Some assets were moved from one column and debits to another column and it all came out looking just like nothing had happened.

One man who did trust me was Paul Vanorden Shaw, a journalist in Rio. He decided to give me his life savings, which amounted to $10,000, to invest. I was really worried whether these guys would know what to do with the money and get a good deal for Shaw. It tuned out they did; Mrs. Shaw later called me after Paul's death to thank me for the wonderful and thoughtful treatment she got from the company. Apparently they'd looked after him and invested his savings well.

I was sent to Juiz da Fora, a small town about 150 miles from Rio, to sell stock. They armed me with a bunch of good leads and I began to pound the pavement. Most people were just curious to see an Americano and listen to my story. Luckily I sold nothing on that trip; many people trusted me but these stocks were worthless.

The Political Scene

In 1953, the country was going through a strange transition. President Getúlio Vargas had been removed from power by the Brazilian Army in 1945, when the military became distrustful of the dictator. In the final days of his power, Vargas had organized two political parties. One, the Brazilian Workers Party (PTB), appealed to the mass of the Brazilian working class while the other, the Social Democratic Party (PSD), was to attract the new middle class. The army feared the anti-Communist populist Vargas might follow Juan Perón of Argentina and set up a workers' republic, and they moved quickly to depose Vargas before that could happen. Brazil returned to democracy and Vargas' former Minister of War, Eurico Dutra, was elected President.

Dutra's presidency (1946–1951) had little effect on the political institutions of the nation. Fifteen years of military dictatorship could not be undone in five years. President Dutra, a lackluster chief executive and incompetent politician, also mismanaged the finances of the country. It was rumored that he governed the country with a copy of the constitution in his hand, but to no avail - the tremendous dollar surpluses built up during the war years were squandered. When Vargas threw his hat into the ring for the presidency in 1950 as the PTB candidate, everyone thought, why not? It was going to be a three-way race with the government apparatus apparently supporting Cristiano Machado, congressman from Minas Gerais, as the PSD candidate. Eduardo Gomes, a popular Air Force general and one of the heroes of the 1922 and 1930 rebellion, led the opposition on behalf of the right-wing UDN (National Democratic Union). He was the idol of the professional and disenfranchised elite of Brazil and appeared to be the most popular candidate. Getúlio Vargas, however, was supported by the majority of the Brazilian electorate. In those days, cynical Brazilians didn't believe that their votes would be counted.

Vargas went on to defeat the two other candidates. It was the first stirring of the Brazilian electorate. This was revolution with a small "r". No one had checked how the majority of the people felt and they apparently liked Vargas. Most people believed that Vargas cleared his candidacy with the Brazilian military and promised to govern democratically, and so now the small guy with cigar in his mouth would be with me again.

My Political Friends

Vargas had assembled his old cronies for his cabinet. For me it felt like home again because Osvaldo Aranha, one of the leaders of the 1930 revolution, was the Minister of Finance and seemed happy to see me. I knew Aranha from the Third Inter American

Conference of Foreign Ministers in Brazil in January 1942. When he inquired how my study of the 1930 Revolution was going, I explained I was in the investment banking business now and writing only at night.

When I had nothing to do I'd go and visit him. I became a familiar sight around the offices of the Ministry of Finance, where Aranha held court. His conversation was always about the revolution. He would call politicians in and they would tell me stories about where they had been in October 1930. The business of state would stack up outside his office. Many a politician would look daggers at me as I left his office smiling or laughing over some funny story or anecdote he had just told me. But when it came to buying shares of what I was selling he was too smart to invest money. He would always promise to buy some shares but he never did. The guys at the office always wondered if I was telling the truth when I said I was going over to talk to the Minister of Finance.

Aranha had collected many documents from the 1930 Revolution and kept them in an office building in downtown Rio. He gave me permission to rummage through these documents and select whatever I wanted for use in a book. I planned to someday write about the Revolution (and I did).

He also suggested that I show my masters thesis to João Neves da Fontoura, then a congressman[61], for his opinion on my portrayal of events. Neves took my thesis and invited me to breakfast the next day. During the breakfast, he handed the thesis back and said, with scathing disdain, "I was the man responsible for the success of the Revolution, not Aranha." Having given Aranha much credit in my thesis, I beat a hasty retreat without saying a word of argument.

One day my curiosity was sparked by an interesting item in the *Jornal do Brasil*, the leading newspaper of Rio de Janeiro, that said Eugênio Gudin Filho[62], Brazil's leading economist at the time, was going to give a talk and analysis of the Brazilian economic situation at the Superior War College. I asked to use the company car, which was a nice sleek black affair. No one was using the car that

---

[61] João Neves da Fontoura was a diplomat, journalist, politician, and author. He was Ministry of Foreign Relations during the Vargas dictatorship and Dutra presidency, and was ambassador to Portugal from 1943 to 1945.

[62] Gudin would go on to become the Minister of Finance under President Café Filho in 1954.

afternoon so off I went. When I arrived, the MP standing at the door gave me a salute and I saluted back. It was reflex action from my days in the army; anyone who gave me a salute I sure as hell would not ignore. In perfect Portuguese I asked the way to the conference. I was so supremely confident that this lecture was open to the public that I took a front row seat. I got my little pad of paper out and settled down to take some notes. Gudin appeared and began his analysis of U.S. economic relations with Brazil.

Soon I noted a rather sharp and undiplomatic tone to his lecture. As he got further into his speech, and I began to squirm at the barbs he was throwing at the U.S.A., it dawned on me that this conference was a by-invitation-only affair. The talk was too frank to have been otherwise. I also realized that the Minister of the Air Force was sitting right beside me. I folded my little note pad and decided to wait until the coffee break to begin a slow exit.

Everyone was enjoying *cafezinhos* - those delightful sweet tiny cups of coffee - as I, trying to look as casual as ever, headed for the door. I almost got out when I bumped into a general I had met many years ago when I was a sergeant in the U.S. army. He was the one who caught the cherries we tossed to make the perfect Manhattan[63]. He seemed surprised to see me, and was I ever surprised to see him! Like any cordial Brazilian - he gave me a big *abraço* and asked what the devil I was doing at the War College. I told him I was working for Chase Bank and that seemed to satisfy him because he just gave me a big smile and told me to show up anytime I wanted to. I wrote a serious report for the company files about the anger of Eugênio Gudin.

One the ways I let off steam was my afternoon visits with José Honório Rodrigues, a noted Brazilian historian who served as director of the National Library. As soon as the stock market closed I would head over to the wonderful Belle Arts building on the Avenida Rio Branco. I climbed those beautiful winding white marble stairs to his office on the top floor. We'd talk about the deplorable state of Brazilian historical studies.

---

[63] See Chapter 9.

Political Developments

By March 1954 politics began to heat up. Carlos Lacerda[64], a crusading newspaperman, kept up a drum beat of attacks on Vargas for corruption. He claimed in his newspaper, *Tribuna da Imprensa*, that Vargas and the people around him were stealing tons of money from the nation. Brazil was, to use his language, living in a "sea of mud." The message began to take effect and many Brazilians grew uneasy with Vargas. Everyone seemed to be part of Lacerda's reforming group, which was called the *Clube da Lanterna.* The tension grew so great that Lacerda decided he needed a bodyguard, and an Air Force colonel volunteered for the job. One night a gunman opened fire in an attempt to assassinate Lacerda and killed the colonel instead. Lacerda was wounded in the leg.

All hell broke loose. The Army, which was unhappy with Vargas, let the Air Force take over the search for the perpetrator of the crime. The Air Force was determined to bring the criminal to justice - no matter where the search led and what it took - and they locked down the city. The Air Force then declared war on the Vargas Administration. There were constant helicopter flights over the city and road blocks as the Air Force sought the killer. The generals made demands on Vargas that he clean up his administration. Then it was discovered that the gunman was paid by the President's chauffeur and Getúlio's personal bodyguard, who was trying to protect Vargas from Lacerda's attacks. Vargas refused to believe the story and fought back. When the military asked that Vargas resign from office he refused.

The irony of the situation was that Vargas had lost an election in 1930 and the army put him in office. In 1954, having won an election, the army wanted him out of the presidency. Vargas dug in his heels and said the only way he would leave office would be if he was dead. The pressures must have been tremendous.

---

64 Carlos Lacerda came from a family of politicians. He attended law school but became a journalist and founded the newspaper *Tribuna da Imprensa* in 1949. In 1947 he was elected to the city council of Rio de Janeiro and in 1950 as a representative for the state of Rio de Janeiro. He and I became close personal friends in the 1960s when he gave a talk to my college class, invited my students to visit Brazil as his guests, and eventually dedicated a public school to my program, called Escola Pace.

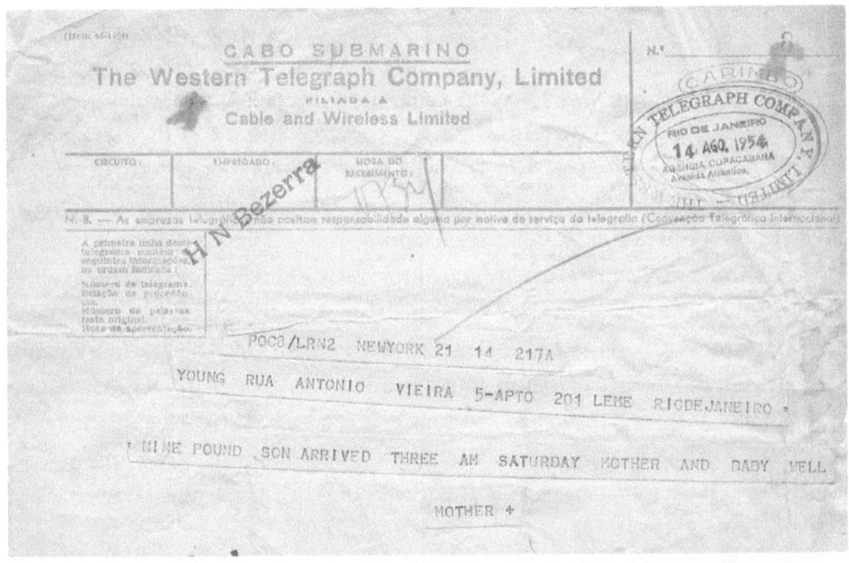

CABO SUBMARINO
The Western Telegraph Company, Limited
FILIADA A
Cable and Wireless Limited

N.º

WESTERN TELEGRAPH COMPANY LIMITED
RIO DE JANEIRO
14 AGO. 1954
AGENCIA COPACABANA
Avenida Atlantica

CIRCUITO | EMPREGADO | HORA DO RECEBIMENTO

H N Bezerra

N. B. — As emprezas telegráficas não aceitam responsabilidade alguma por motivo do serviço da telegrafia (Convenção Telegráfica Internacional)

A primeira linha deste telegrama contém as seguintes informações na ordem indicada: Número do telegrama. Estação de procedência. Número de palavras. Data original. Hora da apresentação.

POC8/LRN2 NEWYORK 21 14 217A
YOUNG RUA ANTONIO VIEIRA 5-APTO 201 LEME RIODEJANEIRO +
NINE POUND SON ARRIVED THREE AM SATURDAY MOTHER AND BABY WELL
MOTHER +

Jordan, Di, and JM.

My Life Changes

Politics and business weren't all I had on my mind, and soon Dionir became pregnant and decided to have the baby in the U.S. We left Rio on August 4, 1954, and flew to New York. I carefully put surgical rubber gloves and scissors in my traveling bag in case the baby arrived while we were en route.

But the baby was slow in coming. Three weeks went by with no baby. Dionir began to get antsy as this was my first job; she urged me to return to Rio. I pleaded with her to let me hang around a few more days, but nothing happened. I went back to Rio on Wednesday night, August 12, but of course she went into labor the next day. Jordan Marten saw the light of day about 2 a.m. on August 14. I was a very proud father, even though I was over 10,000 miles away.

The Suicide of Vargas

At around 4 am on August 24, 1954, Vargas committed suicide. I caught my usual bus for work at 7:45 and at about 8:20 we were in front of the Presidential Palace, the Catete, and the traffic seemed rather slow that day. As we got near the palace someone shouted, "*Vargas se suicidou!*" ("Vargas committed suicide"). The bus erupted with everyone having a different opinion on what had happened. It wasn't the Vargas style to commit suicide. It was a rather drastic act of a politician who died by a heroic gesture. I personally didn't believe a word of it; it was not the Vargas I knew. I continued on to work.

When I got to the office the first thing I did was to listen to the Esso Reporter[65], which carried the morning news on the radio. Sure enough, the reporter was shouting that Vargas had shot himself that morning. I said goodbye to the staff and headed home because I felt there would be trouble in the streets and my ride home might be rough. I got home okay but the sound of the steel gratings coming down over the commercial houses was dramatic. The day itself was so beautiful I decided to go to the beach, as did most of

---

[65] *Repórter Esso*, or the Esso Reporter, was a radio and television news program that followed the style of an American radio program, "Your Esso Reporter." Material for the show was provided by an international news agency out of the U.S.

the *Cariocas* (residents of Rio). There was little or no violence in Rio but the lower middle classes sensed they had lost a leader and followed his body to the airport for its final flight to his birthplace in Rio Grande do Sul. Brazilians did erupt in Porto Alegre, Vargas's home town. This was the end of a chapter of Brazilian history. His long suicide note ended, Serenely I take a first step on my road to eternity and I leave life to enter history." The political manifesto had little effect at the time on the people or the political body.

Did the U.S.A. have anything to do with it? Given the intensity of the Cold War, we may have. Nothing happened anywhere in the world that the CIA didn't play a role in, but how much of a role remains to be seen. This is pure conjecture, but the pressures on Vargas were great and the possibility that Lacerda was on the payroll of the CIA did exist.

Interamericana after Vargas

Life went on. I continued my work at Interamericana and one of the chores was staying in constant contact with the American Embassy. In those days the Embassy was located on Rua Graça Aranha in a lovely, imposing building that seemed to be made of white granite. In the postwar years Americans of all sorts made it their home.

I felt that James S. Kemper, the U.S. ambassador to Brazil, was a good prospect for the sale of Interamericana's securities. After all, he owned the Kemper Insurance Company in the U.S.A. and was a big contributor to the Republican Party. Apparently, these were his only qualifications for the job. At the time, anyone could stroll into the embassy, take the elevator to the 8th floor, and ask if the Ambassador was in with no appointment. As often as not he would see me and we made small talk, but he would not buy any of my offers. I must have impressed him because a few years later he offered me a job managing his insurance company in Brazil.

I wrote articles on the Brazilian stock market for the American language newspaper, the *Brazil Herald*. I'm amazed how little these columns affected public opinion or as a matter of fact how little damage they caused. On March 13, 1955, I was pushing shares of Brahma, major beer company, and noted "that a new high of Cr$700 was reached on March 8." There was no surge of interest by the Brazilian public; my attempts at market manipulation failed.

Jordan and JM in Copacabana.

One day I was selling my stocks when I ran into a man by the name of W.E. Noyes. I can't remember what the occasion was but he asked me what I was doing and I owned up to the fact that I was selling securities. While I gave him my best shot, I did not succeed in selling anything. He did, however, remark that he liked the cut of my jib. Though not quite sure what he meant by this, I listened carefully as he outlined a job offer that I could not turn down: managing the Venezuelan operations of the Diversey Corporation, a small chemical company based out of Chicago. His offer included a dollar salary and a small percentage of the profits. It would mean an eight-month training period in Chicago to familiarize myself with the operations of the corporation. It sounded interesting - but I told him that I did not know anything about chemicals. I was a Ph.D. in history and was not quite sure what I was doing selling stocks. He answered, "Not to worry."

I should have worried, but I accepted his offer. I handed in my resignation and gave the order for everything in the apartment to be packed and sent to Chicago. This included a half-eaten sandwich which someone had left on the dining room table, which was carefully wrapped and shipped.

I left Brazil a bit wistfully. I loved Rio and its soft, messy atmosphere. Rio was an unfinished town and Brazil an unfinished country, but it was remarkably friendly.

Chapter 14. Chemical Plant Manager (1955-56)

This part of my life is hard to tell. There were some highs and some lows, but more lows than highs.

The Diversey Corporation of Chicago was a small chemical company that made Diversol[66], a product that was successful in cleaning farm and food preparation equipment. You could put Diversol into areas to be cleaned and there would be no ill effects for human beings. Milk, beer, Coca-Cola, and, especially in the case of Venezuela, Pepsi-Cola wouldn't have any altered taste. Mr. Noyes, the general manager whom I met in Brazil, had offered me a job with his company. They thought it might be helpful if I knew something about the product I would be manufacturing and selling. As a result, said they would train me for about four months and then turn me loose in

66 Diversol is a cleaner and sanitizer that is still available as of 2014. It is composed of sodium hypochlorite, potassium bromide, and trisodium phosphate.

Venezuela.

In Chicago

Diversey's offices were located on the south side of Chicago, too close, in my opinion, to my old home. Fortunately, they decided to send me out into the field with some of their seasoned veterans to see how they handled sales. I bid goodbye to my bride of little over three years and my now year-old son. I traveled to Iowa and Indiana to watch the old timers and learn how the products were used and sold. The memories of those small farm towns and the tawdriness of the hotels began to get to me. An idea began to grow inside me that this was not a life that I wanted.

I had to sit through training sessions where they taught the new salesmen the product. I remember a session where the instructor said to tell your bit to the customer and summarize it by telling them again, advice I'd remember while teaching at a university.

The salesmen and I lived first in a hotel that was elegant as hell and then moved to Evanston, Illinois, while I learned the business. After about three months, however, they said they couldn't provide the six-month training that I needed for the Venezuela job - I was to have on-the-job training. I had no idea what they were talking about until I was shipped off to Caracas, Venezuela, with about 10,000 pounds of chemicals, a recipe book with instructions on how to mix the product, and the blessings of the corporate headquarters in Chicago.

Onward to Venezuela

The name of my company in Venezuela was Industrias Consolidadas and my factory was in Los Teques, about 20 miles inland from Caracas. The company was robbed the third week I was there. The robbers simply cut through a wall, opened the safe looking for cash, and left. I wonder if they thought a new employee would have brought gold to open the factory.

The fun of the assignment was the complete imbecility of the thing, which fascinated me. The factory resembled a huge shed and I stood on a platform with a huge book in front of me and yelled "*cinco tonelados mezcla*" ("mix 5 tons") and then "*siete libras de B7 mezcla*" ("mix seven pounds of B7") and then the product was ready for market. I was probably a menace to the health of Venezuela.

I began to dislike Venezuela. The whole country was one big company town. You either worked for one of the big five oil companies or you didn't, and the average Venezuelan seemed to hate foreigners. We were called *musiú*, which was a corruption of the French word *monsieur*.

I had to visit brewers to sell Diversol. The most famous one was Heineken and the brew master was Mr. Stienken of Heineken. He made me taste the first day's run as he was proud of his product. I went home smelling like a brewery. It was thirty years before I could stand the taste of beer again.

Another unpleasant aspect of the job was my company's affiliation with the products of the West Disinfectant Company; this was another line of work for which I was unprepared. You know those little white deodorizing blocks that they have in every urinal in the U.S.A.? West also produced a pine-smelling disinfectant that was sold in the supermarkets. I now would have to fight for shelf space at the local supermarket and be on the lookout for possible installation of West products into commercial toilets all over the country. To say the least I found this work very distasteful. In fact, I hated it.

I did get a thrill traveling in the Pepsi-Cola plane, which was a Cessna. I would sit with the pilot up front; the sensation of landing, however, was not so great.

I remember with bitterness the time I discovered that I needed something like 500 tons of caustic soda to manufacture a product and that I could buy it from Japan at about 60% cheaper than I was paying Monsanto Chemical. I proudly announced my finding to the Chicago office only to be told to forget it. They had a sweetheart deal with Monsanto; although I paid them a higher price, the Chicago company got a kickback somewhere along the line. It made competing even harder. Another hard-learned lesson dealt with the three sets of accounting books we kept: one for the American I.R.S., one for the Venezuelan government tax department, and one for the company. I learned so many things that they never taught me in school.

Another rude shock was my huge sale of the product to the Circulo Militar, the military social club. I went confidently to the purchasing agent, who was a lieutenant, and gave him the invoice.

He said there must be some mistake: the price quoted was $10,000 and not the $5,000 I'd stated. I gulped and shook my head, obviously not understanding what was going on. He took me by the hand and led me through the transaction – in a very patient voice, he explained: "Look, you bill me $10,000 for the $5,000 worth of material you deliver and I give you a check for $10,000. You keep $5,000, but of that, you give me $2,500 and you keep $2,500 for yourself." I was now well on my way to understanding how the capitalist system worked.

I cabled headquarters and tried to explain the situation. Though they replied, "Push the product," they immediately sent an accountant down to guide me through the intricacies of the procedure and to relieve me of the $2,500.

Our Life in Venezuela

Our apartment was located on the Avenida Francisco Miranda and had a huge veranda that we shared with the people in the next apartment. There was a low wall between us and our neighbor, who was Hungarian. One weekend, he told me that he'd come back from vacation to find the banks were all closed. He asked if I could loan him 100 bolivars until Tuesday (about $28 in 2013). Hell, he lived next door, and he had such an incredibly sad and believable story that I said sure. When I woke up the next morning, he and his furniture were gone; the family had moved in the middle of the night. Dionir wasn't angry and remarked that they must have needed the money a lot more than we did.

Two American girls worked for Mobil Oil Company in the building and one of them, Helen Sommers, later became a prominent state legislator in Washington State. She seemed so mousy but after she divorced her husband she went into public life[67].

We were living during the Pérez Jiménez dictatorship[68]. Whenever you heard something that sounded like the backfiring of an automobile or gunshot you dropped to the sidewalk just to make sure. Venezuela still worshipped Simon Bolívar, the Liberator of Northern South America. Every hour, the radio station would announce the call letters of the station and the words "*la cuña del libertador*" (the cradle of the Liberator).

There was a nightclub across the street from our apartment that would put loudspeakers outside, blaring out music all night. I went down to the police *delegacia*, to complain. It must have been a hilarious scene - this gringo complaining about not being able to sleep because of loud music. Not surprisingly, the loud music continued.

Dionir and I often visited the oil city of Maracaibo. It was delightfully tropical and it seemed that they had a lot of oil money to spread around. The lake was filled with drilling rigs, and I remember how odd the wells appeared to me when I first saw them scattered all over the lake. At the southern tip of Lake Maracaibo was the quaint old colonial town of San Antonia[69], where time appeared to have stopped in 1783.

There was a quaint but beautiful old home in Caracas that US Steel used as a guest house. I thought it was a private home until I heard the cash register ringing in one of the rooms. Apparently they charged for drinks and other amenities. Just outside of town was an eating place that was very in with the Caracas crowd. It had a cow that would wander through the restaurant and dance floor and everyone would sing "*Tengo una vaca lechera.*" Not very sophisticated.

---

67 Sommers retired at age 75 in 2008, after representing Seattle's 36th Legislative District in the state for 36 years. Prior to her retirement she had served for a decade as chairwoman or co-chair of the House Appropriations Committee of the State of Washington, where she played a pivotal role in writing the state budget.

68 Marcos Evangelista Pérez Jiménez was President and dictator of Venezuela from 1952 to 1958. He headed a corrupt and repressive regime.

69 This town doesn't appear to exist any more.

Time to Leave

Our son Jordan (or JM) was two years old but he still didn't speak. His father spoke English, his mother spoke Portuguese, the maid spoke Spanish, and the children he played with spoke German. He probably thought he needed to make up his own language.

One day I woke up with what appeared to be a flu. When I finally went to a doctor, he informed me that I had picked up yellow jaundice. That did it; Dionir said, "How much money do we have in the bank?" Whatever it was, we considered it enough to pack our bags and return to the U.S.A. I had chills that I couldn't shake and that persisted for at least a week after our return.

I considered myself a failure. I didn't think much of my two-year stint as an investment banker and my one year of managing a small chemical firm, but others in the business world did not share my opinion. We were now going back to the U.S.A. to find work in my chosen field: teaching.

Chapter 15: Professor at Pace College (1956)

Battered and without a clue as what we were going to do, but nonetheless happy, Dionir and I arrived in the United States in August of 1956. I started job hunting and rented an apartment in Long Beach, Long Island - why there, I will never know. It was cheap and it was only for one month, the most miserable month of my life. Our second floor walk-up had a creaky bed that broadcast our lovemaking to the entire neighborhood. The weather turned cold, there was no heat in the apartment, and no jobs were to be found. Trying to get an academic job in August was like trying to get tickets for the World Series the day it started.

Then the phone calls began; people who I had known in Brazil heard that I was unemployed and began calling. One phone call that intrigued me was from former Ambassador James S. Kemper. He was the owner of the Kemper Insurance Company of Chicago, a powerhouse in the Midwest. I had often tried to sell him securities when I was in Brazil working for Chase. He asked if I would be interested in taking over his insurance operations in Brazil and eventually all of Latin America. I thanked him profusely but said that I had decided to be a history professor. He told me that whenever I came to my senses I should give him a call, and he slammed down the phone.

The second call came from the Stanford Research Institute in California. They were looking for someone to develop capital markets in Calcutta, India. Homer Angelo, a businessman I met in

Brazil, was connected to Stanford and offered me that job. Dionir's foot came down on that one real fast. I was intrigued and still a romantic. An investment banker in Calcutta? Wow! But it was not to be.

I did not realize it at the time but I was a hot piece of managerial expertise. Investment banking training in Brazil followed by managing a small chemical company in Venezuela was just what those American corporations were looking for. It didn't matter how competent you were, but I did not know that. Well, maybe I had some idea, but I wanted a teaching job.

Now it was late August and early September. While everyone had already been placed for academic jobs, I made one last desperate stab. When the University of Michigan advertised for a political scientist I applied only to find that the post had already been filled. In desperation I went to the Princeton Placement Service. The lady behind the desk said that she heard a rumor that there was something in New York City at a place called Pace College. She said they were recruiting but that was all she knew about it. What type of school was it? What type of students did they cater to? What was their reputation? To all my questions the answer came back – nothing – nada – zilch.

I took a chance and went to speak to the chair of the Social Science Department, Dr. John "Jack" Flaherty, a smiling pipe-smoking Irishman and a Russian specialist[70]. He seemed pleased to see me but told me that he had employed another Princeton graduate named Harold Lurie just 20 minutes before I walked in. This turned out to be true - he was a Penn graduate and had taught one semester at Princeton. This seemed terribly important at the time.

"Keep in touch," were Dr. Flaherty's final words. Fat chance. Three weeks into September and the semester had already begun. I was desperate. I would've taken anything. Elevator operator, floorwalker, bus driver, you name it. The remark that I never want to hear again as long as I live is "You're overqualified," but I had to

[70] Jack Flaherty got his Ph.D. in European and American history at NYU and then enrolled in the Russian Institute at Columbia University. Later, he became a proponent of Peter Drucker's multi-disciplinary management work. He remained at Pace and became a professor of management.

put some bread in the mouth of my baby and the times demanded that I get a job.

I decided to throw in the towel and go crawling back to Chase Bank. The subway stop that let me off for the Chase Bank happened to be directly in front of Pace College and I thought to myself, "What the hell, give it one last whirl." I went to say hello to Dr. Flaherty on the 14th floor. He greeted me like a long lost brother and asked, "Where the devil have you been? We've been looking all over New York for you. Can you teach Modern European History?"

"Sure," I responded breathlessly. "And can you teach American History, both the early and modern periods?" My prompt answer was "Sure thing!" And, "Can you teach Ancient History? By this I mean the early Christian period." That stumped me a bit but my answer was a "Sure!" anyway. "And a course in American Government?" I was not sure what that was but in my condition if he had asked if I could teach a course on Indonesian politics the answer would have been, "Yes! Yes! and yes again!"

As nothing was said about Latin America, I kept my mouth shut. And so in 1956 I started my career at Pace College.

Dr. Flaherty added as an afterthought as the semester had gotten underway that I audit the classes of one of the professors of ancient history. I did. That was a big mistake. The professor, Dr. Joseph Sinzer[71], had a deep rolling voice and was a perfect double of a famous New York City Catholic spokesman by the name of Msg. Fulton J. Sheen. Every lecture by Sinzer was a dramatic reproduction of Msg. Sheen. Prof. Sinzer's voice was mellow and resonant and the man was a natural actor. The drama that he brought into the classroom was pure ham. But the students sat transfixed as Christ was nailed to the cross. I sat and slowly slumped in my seat in the back of the classroom. "No way would I be able to handle this," I said to myself.

After class I promptly called Dr. Flaherty and I quit before there was more blood on the table. Dr. Flaherty pleaded with me. He was desperate. "Please give it a try!" he begged, and I did. I handled everything well except the ancient history course. When I came to Jesus Christ I was a disaster. I was an agnostic leaning

[71] Dr. Sinzer became the academic vice president of Pace University NYC and served as the C. Richard Pace Professor of History.

toward atheism, so I gave them the historical Jesus Christ. This was 1956 and some Catholic Jesuit high school kids in the class knew that I was bluffing. I managed to insult every faith in the class, the Catholics, the Protestants, and the Jews. If I were to teach today I'd end up insulting the Muslims as well. They let me finish the semester but I never taught early Christianity again.

Teaching at Pace was an experience never to be forgotten. I had to climb down from the ivory tower of an elite university to the rough and tumble of a metropolitan college that catered to a first generation of students to attend a school of higher education. They didn't care where I had my degree from but they did care whether or not I knew my material. Ties and jackets were mandatory and we were ordered to take attendance and report tardiness (at least until the 1970's rolled in when all this would disappear).

Soon I was able to introduce a Latin American history course and finally a course in Brazilian Civilization. I was fascinated to see the growing interest in Brazil.

We moved several times after I got the job, first to Glen Cove, Long Island and then to Rego Park, Queens, where there was a United Nations enclave. Dionir didn't want to bring up children in New York City and Long Island felt like a dead end. We drew a circle around the city. Mrs. Dana Munroe, the wife of my old Princeton professor, suggested that we consider living near Princeton, so we found a house in Kendall Park, N.J., near Princeton and eventually built a house in Princeton itself.

Epilogue

My career at Pace College, then Pace University, continued for 42 years and involved visits to governors, presidents, and many trips to the Amazon. I was one of the first Brazilianists in America and developed a course in Brazilian civilization, teaching how that country's culture differed from our own and from the rest of Latin America.

Although my first love has always been teaching, I also published three books:

- *The Brazilian Revolution of 1930 and the Aftermath* (Rutgers University Press, 1966)
- *Brazil 1954-64: End of a Civilian Cycle* (Facts on File, 1972)
- *Brazil Emerging World Power* (Krieger Books, 1982)

I hope to write a second volume about the development of Brazilian studies in the U.S.

Index

www.ingramcontent.com/pod-product-compliance
Ingram Content Group UK Ltd.
Pitfield, Milton Keynes, MK11 3LW, UK
UKHW040602210726
13854UKWH00008B/1833